Island Hopping in New England

Island Hopping in New England

by Mary Maynard

YANKEE BOOKS

A division of
Yankee Publishing Incorporated
Dublin, New Hampshire

All photographs by the author
except where otherwise noted.

Designed by Jill Shaffer

Yankee Publishing Incorporated
Dublin, New Hampshire 03444

First Edition

Library of Congress Catalog Card Number 85-51871
ISBN 0-89909-091-5

CONTENTS

MAINE *continued*

MAPS

INTRODUCTION

Islands are very special places. Each has a character all its own. And the islands found off the shores of New England are a diverse and special group indeed.

Carved out and separated from the mainland at the whim of reckless glaciers pushing down from the Arctic during the Ice Age, literally thousands of small landforms dot the coastal waters of New England. Most of these islands lie off the coast of Maine, and their numbers dwindle as you move south along the shores of New Hampshire, Massachusetts, Rhode Island, and Connecticut. Inland Vermont, bordering beautiful Lake Champlain, has a select group of islands all its own.

Gulls will let you know when you travel too near their nests on New Hampshire's Star Island.

Archaeologists and historians tell us that centuries ago Indians were the first inhabitants of the islands, using them as summer camping and fishing grounds. Signs of what many believe to be Viking exploits, dating from the eleventh century, have been discovered on some islands. Later came the European explorers, most of whom stopped at the islands only long enough to name them, often after themselves.

A few very early permanent European settlements, however, are known to have existed on the islands, some predating mainland settlements. On Matinicus, about fifteen miles offshore and twenty miles out from Rockland, Maine, are the remains of old stone houses, believed to have been built by French fishermen. And the Pilgrims who arrived at Plymouth were greeted by the Indian Samoset, dressed in an odd assortment of European garments and speaking English, which he had learned from fishermen on Maine's Monhegan Island, where his tribe, the Pemaquids, spent their summers.

As English and French colonies were established on the mainland, some of the more adventurous fishermen and farmers and their families moved out to the islands, lured by tales of bountiful fishing grounds and grazing pastures. These families lived a rugged, often lonely existence, with few conveniences and virtually no communication with the mainland.

During the nineteenth century, the islands became havens for summer visitors, or "rusticators" as the natives called them, who had discovered the healthful, tangy salt air and relaxing style of island living. But rusticators could not live without conveniences or communication with the mainland, and soon roads, well-built cottages, indoor plumbing, electricity, and telephones came to some islands. Thus, island tourism was born.

Within a short time artists and poets followed, paying homage through words and pictures to the mystical beauty of these curiously enticing remote patches of sand and rock. Henry Wadsworth Longfellow, John Greenleaf Whittier, Robert Tristram Coffin, Harriet Beecher Stowe, Edna St. Vincent Millay, and Sarah Orne Jewett are just a few of the New England writers who fell under the islands' spell and wrote passionately about them. In the early 1920s, poet Rachel Field penned the oft-repeated lines, "If once you have slept on an island/ You'll never be quite the same." Several Maine islands have claimed these lines as a motto.

Some of Connecticut's tiny Thimble Islands accommodate but a single structure, such as this "high-rise" on Exton's Reef.

Today it is possible for the day-tripper to hop aboard a ferry in the morning, spend the day exploring, biking, and picnicking on an island, and be home in time for dinner. And during the summer, you can take a ferry to certain islands, such as Islesford (Little Cranberry), Maine, just for dinner!

The New England islands offer places to explore, to be inspired, or simply to escape to. For the naturalist, there are uninhabited preserves, such as the Parker River National Wildlife Refuge on Massachusetts' Plum Island. Here in the spring you can view the nesting grounds of migratory waterfowl. As many as three hundred bird species have been sighted here throughout the year. For the escapist, there's the serenity of an antique rocker on the expansive wraparound porch of either the Surf Hotel on Block Island (Rhode Island) or the Chebeague Inn in Casco Bay (Maine), where you can watch a spectacular sunrise or sunset. And those who think island living is just a bit too bucolic for their taste will be happy to know that you can find everything from a Jacuzzi to jazz on such "stylish" islands as Nantucket and Martha's Vineyard off the coast of Massachusetts.

There are islands for biking, hiking, rock climbing, birding, camping, shelling, hunting, fishing, clamming, swimming, snorkeling, sailing, golf, and tennis. You can search for buried treasure or attend a religious conference, and the perennial student can take courses in marine biology for college credit or seafood cooking just for fun.

You'll find opportunities for old-fashioned pleasures such as croquet, horseshoes, stargazing, pie-eating contests, bag races, and square-dancing. You can attend a band concert or a symphony, a poetry reading or a sing-along. Whatever your pleasure, the islands of New England have something for you.

But to the uninitiated, a few words of warning: Heed the words of Rachel Field. These islands cast a spell that is apt to haunt you forever. Anyone who has ever slept on Star Island will tell you of the bewitching chant that is called out to you as you sail away from the dock: "You *will* come back! You *will* come back!" And most do.

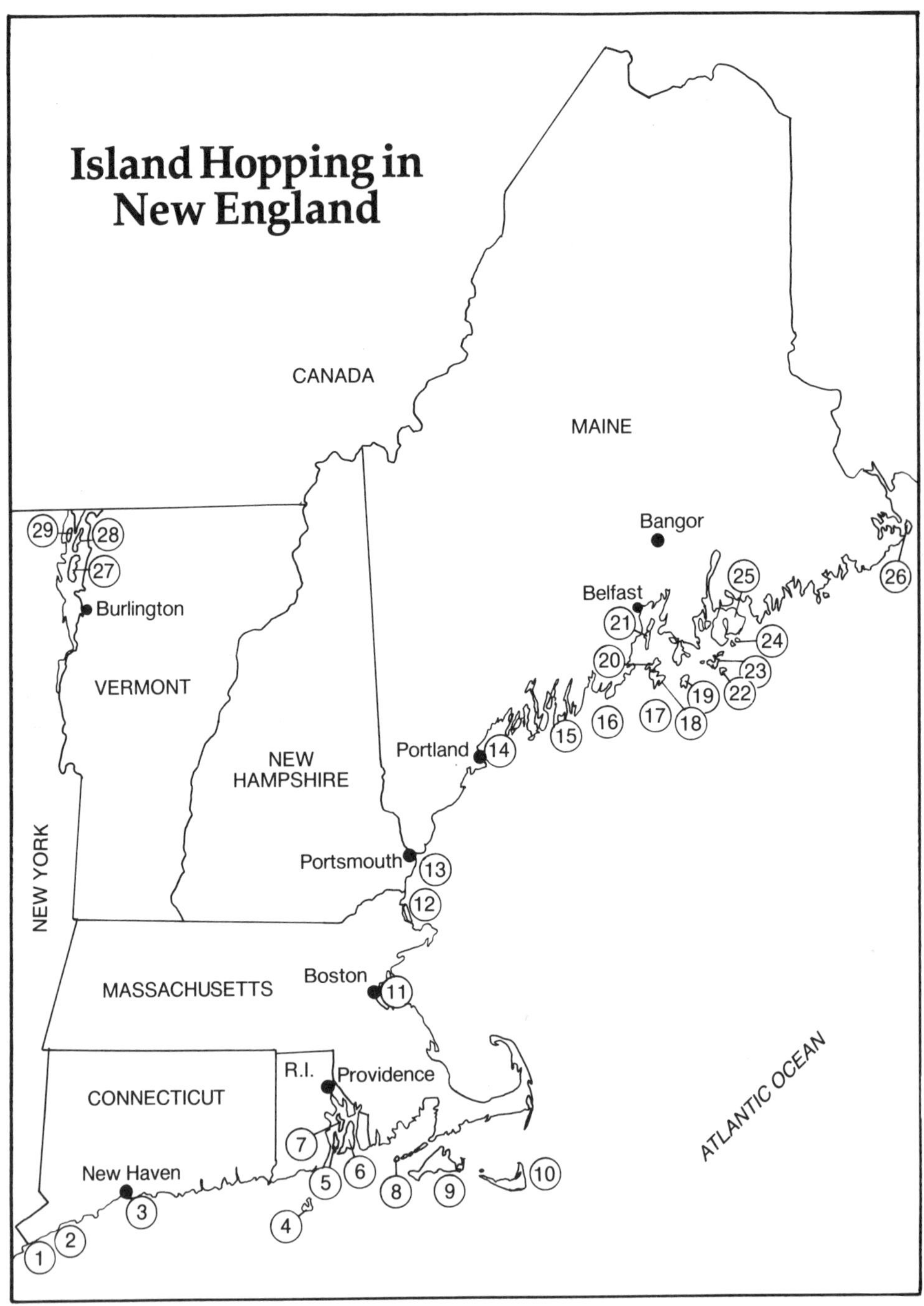
Island Hopping in New England
CANADA
MAINE
Bangor
Belfast
VERMONT
Burlington
NEW HAMPSHIRE
Portland
Portsmouth
NEW YORK
MASSACHUSETTS
Boston
R.I.
Providence
CONNECTICUT
New Haven
ATLANTIC OCEAN
1
2
3
4
5
6
7
8
9
10
11
12
13
14
15
16
17
18
19
20
21
22
23
24
25
26
27
28
29

Islands At-a-Glance

Key S — seasonal
Y — year-round

	MAP LOCATION	PASSENGER FERRY	CAR FERRY	CRUISE BOAT	AIRLINES	HOTEL/INN	CAMPING	RESTAURANT	FOOD/STORE	PICNICKING	GUIDED TOURS	MUSEUM/HIST. SOCIETY	HIKING TRAILS	BIRD WATCHING	BIKING TRAILS	BIKE RENTAL	BOAT RENTAL	SWIMMING	FISHING	HUNTING	TENNIS	GOLF	GIFT SHOPS
Aquidneck (Bridge)	6			S	Y	Y	S	Y	Y	Y	S	Y	Y	Y	Y	Y	S	S	Y	S	Y	S	Y
Bailey/Orr's (Bridge)	14	S		S		Y		Y	Y	Y		S	Y	Y	Y		S	S	Y				S
Block	4	Y	Y	S	Y	Y		Y	Y	Y	Y	S	Y	Y	Y	S	S	S	Y		S		S
Boston Harbor Islands	11	S		S			S		S	S	S	S	S	S				S	S				S
Calf	1						S			S			S	S				S	S				
Campobello (Bridge)	26	S				S	S	S	Y	Y	S	S	Y	Y	Y			S	Y			S	S
Capitol (Bridge)	15			S		S				S			S	S				S	S				
Captain	2	S		S					S	S				S				S	S				
Conanicut (Bridge)	5			S		S	S	Y	Y	Y		S	Y	Y	Y			S	Y	S	S	S	Y
Cranberry	24	Y		S				S	Y	Y		S	Y	Y	Y			S	Y				S
Damariscove	15			S						S	S		S	S				S	S				
Eagle	14			S						S	S	S		S				S	S				
Elizabeth	8	Y			Y	S		S	S	Y		S	Y	Y	Y		S	S	Y				S
Frenchboro	22	Y	Y							Y		S	Y	Y				S	Y				
Great & Little Diamond	14	Y		S						S				Y				S	S				
Hurricane	18									S	S			S				S	S				
Isle au Haut	19	Y		S			S		S	Y	S		Y	Y	Y			S	Y				
Isle La Motte (Bridge)	29			S		S	S	S	Y	Y		S	Y	Y	Y			S	Y	S			S
Isles of Shoals	13	S		S		S		S	S	S	S	S	S	S				S	S				S
Islesboro	21	Y	Y	S	Y	S		S	Y	Y		Y	Y	Y	Y			S	Y		S	S	S
Little & Great Chebeague	14	Y		S		S		S	S	Y			Y	Y	Y			S	Y			S	S
Martha's Vineyard	9	Y	Y	S	Y	Y	S	Y	Y	Y	S	Y	Y	Y	Y	S	S	S	Y	S	S	S	Y
Matinicus/Criehaven	17	Y	Y		Y				Y	Y			Y	Y				S	Y				S
Monhegan	16	Y		S		S		S	Y	Y	S	S	Y	Y				S	Y				S
Mount Desert (Bridge)	25			S	Y	Y	S	Y	Y	Y	S	Y	Y	Y	Y	S	S	S	Y		S	S	Y
Nantucket	10	Y	Y	S	Y	Y		Y	Y	Y	S	Y	Y	Y	Y	S	S	S	Y		S	S	Y
North Haven	20	Y	Y	S	Y	Y	S	S	Y	Y		S	Y	Y	Y	S	S	S	Y		S	S	S
North Hero (Bridge)	28	Y	Y	S		S	S	S	Y	Y			Y	Y	Y			S	Y	S			S
Norwalk	2			S			S			S	S		S	S				S	S				
Peaks	14	Y	Y	S		Y		Y	Y	Y	Y	S	Y	Y	Y	S		S	Y				S
Plum (Bridge)	12				S			S	S	Y			Y	Y	Y			S	Y	S			S
Prudence	7	Y	Y	S		S	S	S	Y	Y	S	S	Y	Y	Y			S	Y	S			S
Squirrel	15	Y		S									S	S									S
South Hero/Grand (Bridge)	27	Y	Y	S		S	S	S	Y	Y		S	Y	Y	Y			S	Y	S			Y
Swans	23	Y	Y			S		S	Y	Y		S	Y	Y	Y			S	Y				S
Thimble Islands	3	S		S										S									
Vinalhaven	18	Y	Y	S	Y	Y		Y	Y	Y	Y	Y	Y	Y	Y	S		S	Y				S

GENERAL INFORMATION

Getting There

While sailing off to an island on your own private yacht may be considered the first-class way to go, to do so (and providing you have the yacht) would be missing half the fun.

The New England islands are tied to the mainland by a vintage fleet of ferryboats, or "water taxies," that shuttle back and forth as regularly and dependably as the ebb and flow of the tide. Carrying everything from groceries to the U.S. mail, and from flats of petunias to newly repaired window screens — along with day-trippers and islanders, of course — the ferries provide a trip that is an adventure in and of itself.

Islanders are, for the most part, eager to tell you about "their" islands. Generally you will get more information, history, and folklore from an islander on a one-hour ferry ride than from any other source.

Bailing water from small boats is one way kids in Rhode Island's Jamestown earn their ice cream money.

The captains of the ferries rate a chapter of their own. Jimmy Barstow, for instance, who pilots the *Laura B.* out of Port Clyde, Maine, to Monhegan Island, may have grown up in New York City, but you won't find a more knowledgeable, capable, or affable young skipper along the coast. Among a few of the passengers who have preferred the *Laura B.* over a private yacht are John F. Kennedy, Zero Mostel, Rockwell Kent, and Jamie Wyeth.

Most of the ferries will carry you and your bicycle to an island, but only a few take cars. For the ones that do take cars (which can be expensive), it is almost always essential to make reservations well in advance for both the outgoing and the return trips.

If you plan to drive your car to a ferry landing, you also must be mindful that parking facilities are at a premium. Most ferries are tied up at docks in small, densely populated harbors that leave little or no room for parking lots. Parking facilities are usually located somewhere within walking distance, but it's wise to look into this in advance. If you plan

Maine's Islesboro offers some of New England's best sunset views.

to catch the ferry from Woods Hole, Massachusetts, to Martha's Vineyard, for example, you have to park your car several miles away and take the shuttle bus to the ferry landing.

The passenger rates vary from ferry to ferry, but they are generally quite reasonable. Taking a car, bicycle, or excess luggage will, of course, incur an additional fee. Animals can be taken aboard but they must be securely leashed or caged at all times.

For most New England islands, you'll find you need nothing more in the way of transportation than a good pair of walking shoes. Many islands, such as Cuttyhunk (Massachusetts), Prudence (Rhode Island), Monhegan (Maine), and Star (New Hampshire), can easily be traversed in a single day or less.

For those who are prone to *mal de mer*, several of the islands have airline services. These services are listed in the individual island descriptions.

A few of the islands covered in this book are connected to the mainland by bridge. Purists might disdain such places as having lost their island status because of such connections. But often these islands, such as Conanicut (Rhode Island), have managed to retain their independence and individuality, two of the "special" qualities indigenous to islands.

Among the many treats at the Apple Farm Market in Vermont's South Hero are delicious apple cider doughnuts.

Accommodations

Island accommodations range from nonexistent or barely adequate on uninhabited islands to rustically charming and luxurious on islands with year-round communities.

The larger islands have almost everything the mainland has to offer in the way of lodgings, in addition to unrivaled sunrises and sunsets. The Island Inn on Monhegan, for instance, lets you choose a room with a "sea-sunset" view or one with a "meadow-sunrise" view.

Some of the smaller islands have a single family-run hotel that has been dispensing hospitality for several generations. You may have to share the bath and, in some cases, to depend on old-time gas and kerosene lamps, but your reward usually will be scrumptious dining on the catch-of-the-day while overlooking a tranquil, picturesque harbor.

Some of the best cooks (you rarely hear an island cook referred to as a chef) ply their trade at island inns and guesthouses. Many of them grow their own vegetables and herbs right outside the kitchen door. And not far from that same door they have their daily choice of freshly caught fish and lobsters. Breads and pastries are home-baked, often with island-grown fruits and berries.

Guesthouses are popular island retreats, but due to frequent changes in ownership, they are difficult to keep track of. Real estate agents or general stores are the best sources of information on these. Another good bet is to ask the ferry service personnel. They generally know who is renting rooms during any given season.

It is necessary to make advance reservations for overnight accommodations on any island in any season, and you should make them well in advance during the summer months. Many hotels and guesthouses suspend operations for the winter, and the ferry schedule to most islands is reduced as well.

Bicycles and mopeds are available for rent on a few of the islands, but they are snatched up quickly. To avoid being disappointed, particularly on a day trip, bring your own.

When you are using a bicycle or a moped be sure to stick to designated paths and roads. This not only will help you to avoid an accident (sand and gravel can be treacherous under wheels), but is essential to protecting the island environment. Erosion is a serious problem, and tires can do much damage to plants and soil that keep the island ecology intact.

Camping is permitted on some islands, but be prepared to adhere to strictly enforced regulations. Fires are a constant threat to fragile island ecologies and must be guarded against at all times.

Many of the islands have cottages for rent by the week, month, or season. These can be checked out through a local real estate agent, and sometimes notices are posted in the country store or whatever public building is nearest to the dock.

Local chambers of commerce also are a good source of information for accommodations and tourist attractions. Addresses and telephone numbers for many of these appear in the chapters on individual islands.

Day-tripping

If you are day-tripping or camping on one of the small, less-inhabited islands, you may have to bring your own food. While most of the islands have at least a general store or snack bar, the food, which had to be "imported" to begin with, is usually expensive. Some enterprising young people run very profitable lemonade and cookie stands in the summer along the roadside.

Public rest room facilities on the islands are in short supply. Most campsites have a few compost or outhouse toilets and a pump for drinking water. If there is ferry service to the island, rest rooms usually are located near the dock.

A cardinal rule on all the islands is this: Whatever you bring with you to the island, take it with you when you leave. Never leave trash behind. Nothing creates hostility among the natives more quickly than finding their beautiful island littered with cans and plastic bags. Islanders, who are generally friendly hosts, are fiercely protective of their land and are obliged to enforce rigid standards. Everyone should respect these standards in order to preserve the islands' beauty and uniqueness.

Most of the property on the islands is privately owned, and "No Trespassing" signs must be observed. Public beaches and picnic areas usually are well-marked.

You can often obtain a map of an island at the island store. Trails, campsites, picnic grounds, and

New England lighthouses, like this one on Massachusetts' Nantucket, enjoy a long and rich history.

other public facilities, as well as historical attractions, are shown.

Quite a few of the islands have small museums or libraries with island artifacts on display. Unfortunately, these places are open only a few days a week and for a limited number of hours. If you are particularly interested in visiting such places, you'll have to call ahead to get their schedules. Most of them depend on volunteer help, which is hard to come by on a sunny day, particularly on one of these beautiful islands.

Although the summer season is generally considered the best time to visit the New England islands (in some cases it may be the only time to visit), some islands offer year-round activities and accommodations. The spring and fall seasons are particularly peaceful and uncrowded, and excellent times for exploring nature trails, walking deserted beaches, or bicycling along uncongested roads. Most accommodations offer greatly reduced rates at this time of year. Winter, too, can be enjoyable on some islands. Cross-country skiing, ice skating, and many other activities are offered, and quite often the shallow waters surrounding the islands keep the temperature a few degrees warmer than that of the mainland.

CONNECTICUT

The old heave-ho! Young sailors learn the ropes aboard a Schooner Inc. research vessel.

The Connecticut coastline, entirely bordering Long Island Sound, was spared some of the indiscriminate ravagings of the ancient glaciers that gave rise to New England's many islands. Unlike the ragged and rock-strewn coast of Maine, for example, Connecticut's two-hundred-fifty-mile coastline is largely made up of gently sloping beaches, crescent-shaped bays, and calm, protected harbors. The state's islands, sprinkled along the sound, are relatively small, few in number, and close to the shore. (One of the sound's large islands, Fishers, discovered by Adriaen Block in 1614 and settled by John Winthrop, Jr., in 1644, was officially declared the property of New York in 1879, although it is only a few miles off the Connecticut shore. It is still serviced by a ferry that leaves from New London, Connecticut.)

Connecticut's islands tend to be clustered in small groups, such as the two Calf Islands, the three Captain Islands, the sixteen Norwalk Islands, and the largest and most popular group, the Thimble Islands, numbering more than three hundred. Almost all the inhabitable islands are now privately owned, while many others have been preserved as wildlife sanctuaries. Some, however, still offer free access (provided you have your own boat) to fine swimming beaches, nature trails, and, in a few cases, primitive campsites.

Probably the best way to see these islands and to learn about them is to take one of the daily cruise boats that ply the waters around them. The loquacious sea captains of the *Volsunga III*, the *Sea Mist*, and *The Lady Joan* will delight you with colorful stories, some amusing anecdotes, a bit of history, and lots of local gossip. If you're really captivated, you may want to try renting one of these island homes for a week, a month, or the season. According to one local real estate agent, most owners tend to rent only to family members or friends, but each summer a few houses do come on the open market as rentals. You can expect to pay two or three thousand dollars a month for renting a small cottage and considerably more for a larger one.

Norwalk Islands

Connecticut may have lost the battle with New York over Fishers Island, but it won the dispute over possession of the Norwalk Islands. There are sixteen in all (not a bad trade-off!), and they have changed little since 1614 when Dutch explorer Adriaen Block first sighted them.

Nathan Hale, the courageous patriot and spy whose only regret was that he had "but one life to lose for my country," left these islands on his final, fateful mission for General George Washington.

These islands, with a rich history and a promising future, cover a six-mile stretch and range in size from less than an acre to almost seventy acres. They extend from just east of the Westport-Norwalk town line to the waters off Darien. While most of the islands are privately owned, a few, such as Shea, Grassy, and Cockenoe, are owned by adjoining coastal towns. Others, such as Chimon, considered by conservationists to be the most beautiful and valuable (there is an important heron rookery here), are national wildlife refuges. During the past several years local and national groups have tried to create legislation that would insure the protection of these islands by acquiring them for The Nature Conservancy. The Nature Conservancy is a national conservation organization involved in the preservation of 2.4 million acres throughout the country. It owns and manages a national system of nearly eight hundred sanctuaries, many of them located on islands.

The Norwalk Indians, the first to fish off these islands, are credited with the discovery of oysters in this region. The remains of Indian graves on Wilson Point at the entrance to Wilson's Cove are packed with oyster shells, and to this day Norwalk fishermen are proud of their long tradition of having one of the finest oyster industries in the United States.

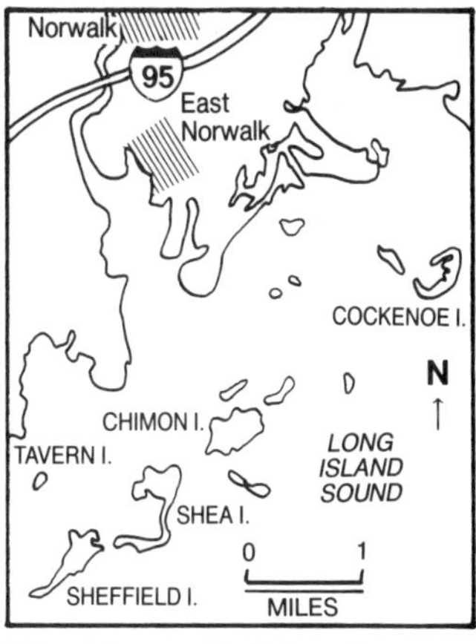

The Norwalk Islands

During the Revolutionary War the islands were strategic hiding places for men and ships. Nathan Hale, the courageous patriot and spy whose only regret was that he had "but one life to lose for my country," left these islands on his final, fateful mission for General George Washington. American whaleboats sought refuge among the inlets and shoals after making forays into Long Island Sound to harass British ships. The whaleboats could easily retreat behind the shoals where the larger British ships dared not venture. During Prohibition rum runners and smugglers took advantage of the same secluded spots to carry on their illegal activities. Small fishing boats would rendezvous in the Atlantic with larger vessels carrying cargoes of rum from the Caribbean islands. Captains of the fishing boats would load their holds with the illegal bottles and then, under the guise of fishing, craftily weave in and out among the islands, usually outwitting the patrol boats. Their booty eventually would be secretly deposited on the mainland, bringing them a much more lucrative price than a boatload of fish.

In later years, because of the islands' proximity to New York's Broadway, many theatrical personalities sought out the solitude of the Norwalk Islands. **Tavern Island** particularly was a haven for some, including playwright Lillian Hellman, who wrote *The Little Foxes* there, and producer Billy Rose, who built himself a showplace complete with exotic birds and animals and filled with priceless works of art. All that remains of his estate today is the crumbling statuary of five Grecian maidens.

Cockenoe (pronounced ko-KEY-nee) **Island** and its well-protected harbor have long been popular recreational spots for boaters. Wide sandy beaches, clam flats at low tide, picnic areas, and

SAUGATUCK VALLEY AUDUBON SOCIETY

Bird and botany lovers head for shore at Cockenoe Island during one stopover in Conservator's *six-hour island tour.*

campgrounds provide lots of activity. The town of Westport, which owns the island, permits campfires here, and along with regular barbecues, a favorite dinner menu on Cockenoe (borrowed from the Norwalk Indians) is freshly dug clams cooked in seawater on an open fire. So popular is this activity that all summer long mainlanders looking out across the harbor can see myriad tiny flickering lights from the many campfires rimming the island.

Shea Island, owned by Norwalk and covered with berries and wildflowers, is another popular camping spot and also has a good beach and picnic area. Use of some of the facilities on these islands is restricted to residents, so it's best to check with the local chamber of commerce in advance. Local residents hope that a ferry eventually will make regularly scheduled trips to the islands.

Several cruise boats, including ***The Lady Joan*** and the ***Long Island Queen,*** provide ample opportunities to view the islands from a distance and to learn more about their history and traditions. ***Conservator,*** owned and operated by the Saugatuck Valley Audubon Society, takes groups and individuals on explorations of some of the islands.

On a typical six-hour cruise aboard the *Conservator* (a flat-bottomed catamaranlike vessel), you'll get to see at least four islands (usually including Chimon, Sheffield, and Shea). The boat, which carries about eighteen passengers, stops to let you explore each island. A professional guide will assist you in identifying such things as prickly pear cactus, shadbush, peppergrass, beach plum, and poison ivy (in case you don't recognize it). Bird watchers will be happy to know that on an average day more than thirty species of birds, including oystercatchers and snowy egrets, have been sighted. The trips run from early May through mid-October and are very reasonably priced.

The Lady Joan offers a one-and-a-half-hour tour of the islands aboard a replica of a Mississippi riverboat. The captain directs your attention to various islands along the way, describing historical points of interest on each and sharing local lore. Snacks and beverages are available aboard the boat.

Bird watchers will be happy to know that on an average day more than thirty species of birds, including oystercatchers and snowy egrets, have been sighted.

ACCESS

NORWALK. Directions: From I-95 (Connecticut Turnpike) take exit 14 (traveling north) or exit 15 (traveling south).

THE LADY JOAN and ***LONG ISLAND QUEEN.*** **Directions:** From I-95 take exit 16 (East Avenue). Turn left (south) on East Avenue, following signs to Cove Marina. **Season:** July 1 through Labor Day. **Admission:** Charged. **Telephone:** (203) 838-9003.

CONSERVATOR. **Directions:** From I-95 take exit 16 to Route 136, which will bring you to Veterans Park in East Norwalk. Follow signs to boat landing. **Season:** May through October. **Admission:** Charged. **Telephone (Saugatuck Valley Audubon Society):** (203) 866-7830.

CHAMBERS OF COMMERCE. Norwalk: P.O. Box 668, Norwalk, CT 06854; (203) 866-2521. **Westport:** P.O. Box 30, Westport, CT 06881; (203) 227-9234.

Captain Islands

Greenwich, Connecticut, is such a classy town! It has its very own islands for swimming, sunbathing, volleyball, and kite-flying. It even has two small ferryboats that do nothing all summer but shuttle residents back and forth between the mainland and these island beaches. While the ferry service is primarily for residents, guests at the local inns may ride them as well.

On the charts the islands are called The Captains, but to the local gentry they're known as Beach Islands. There are three islands in all, Great Captain, Little Captain, and Wee Captain. Great and Little Captains, with their acres of sandy shores and beach grass, are open to the public, while Wee Captain is privately owned.

Great Captain, consisting of eighteen acres, has a nice bathing beach along with a pavilion that houses a concession stand, rest rooms, and showers. Its half-mile length makes it just about the right size for jogging or beachcombing. On the island's southeast side stands an attractive hewn-granite light-

The deck of The Presidents *has played host to three chief executives: Truman, Eisenhower, and Kennedy.*

house built in the early 1880s. It is now the home of the island caretaker, the light having long since been replaced by an automatic blinker. **Little Captain,** which also has a fine beach and bathhouses, is a popular gathering spot for those with small children. It's easy to keep track of them here, and they have plenty of other children with whom to build sandcastles.

Both of these islands were at one time privately owned amusement and entertainment centers. Great Captain had a large private beach club on it that contained, among other things, a ballroom with a huge orchestra pit, attracting some of the widely known Big Bands of the day, and a dining salon with an elaborate multicolored lighting system. Little Captain had an amusement park complete with a merry-go-round and a dancing pavilion. Several disastrous fires and the Depression of the 1930s put an end to these attractions, however, and both islands now are run by the Greenwich Parks and Recreation Commission for town residents and their guests.

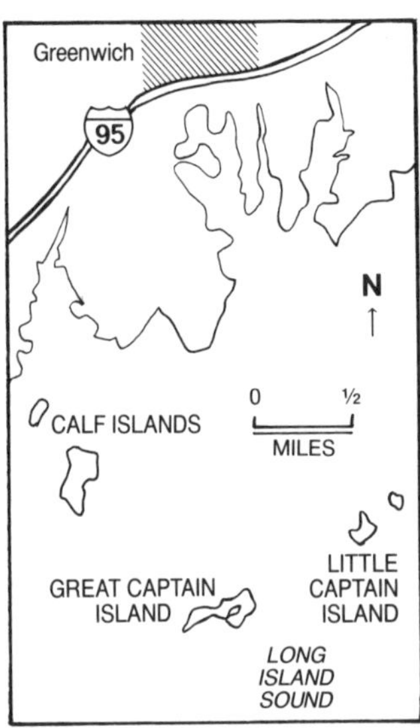

The Captain Islands and Calf Islands

If you really want to cruise these islands in style, you can charter the nifty little ninety-three-foot yacht tied up at the Showboat Inn dock just across from the ferry dock in Greenwich. Formerly known as *Patricia* and *Honey-Fitz,* it is now called ***The Presidents,*** and it's here where Truman tickled the ivories, Ike drove a few golf balls off the stern, and JFK threw a birthday bash for Jackie. The yacht is available for charters (at megabuck prices, of course), but you can enjoy a little snooping for free from the dock. You can view the beautifully maintained upper deck along with the semiopen fore and aft decks where the presidents entertained their famous guests. You can peer into the plush beige and white main deck salon but not the double stateroom. The yacht was designed with only one stateroom so that no guests could be asked to stay overnight.

The **Showboat Inn and Restaurant,** a full-service motor inn located right in Greenwich Harbor, also offers the ***Dixie Belle*** for charters. A replica of a small Mississippi paddle wheeler, it would be great for a children's birthday party.

Calf Islands

The two Calf Islands are closer to shore than the Captains. Located about a mile from the main-

GREENWICH YMCA

Sailors leave the shore at Southern Calf Island to take on the challenge of the open waters.

land, they are just west of the entrance to Greenwich Harbor. Northern Calf, the smaller of the two, is privately owned. **Southern Calf,** connected to its sibling by a sandbar, is a twenty-eight-acre island owned and operated by the Greenwich YMCA. During the summer the Y maintains a day camp for local youths here, but on weekends from mid-May through Labor Day the facilities are open to the public. Several family- and adult-oriented programs are offered, including sailing, navigating, and racing lessons (the Y owns an extensive fleet of various types of sailboats), New England clambakes, and pig-roast luaus.

The island has a sandy beach, picnic area (tables and stoves), playground (sports equipment available to groups), nature and hiking trails, campsites (some with floors), showers, rest rooms, and a first-aid station. It is accessible by private boat (nominal docking fee). You can also rent almost the entire island for the weekend. For about five hundred dollars charter groups are given exclusive use of the island's picnic shelter with an attached kitchen (complete with sink, stove, oven, and restaurant-size refrigerator) as well as the use of campsites, tents, and a generator for electricity. For a small additional charge, the Y will even provide leadership for children's activities.

You can rent almost the entire island for the weekend.

ACCESS

GREENWICH. Directions: From I-95 (Connecticut Turnpike) take exit 3 in Greenwich.

BEACH (CAPTAIN) ISLAND FERRY. Directions: From exit 3 off I-95 follow Steamboat Road to the town dock. **Season:** June through Labor Day. **Admission:** Charged. **Telephone (Parks and Recreation Commission):** (203) 622-7814.

GREENWICH YMCA. For all information and reservations for Southern Calf Island, write to the Greenwich YMCA, Calf Island Office, 50 East Putnam Avenue, Greenwich, CT 06830; (203) 869-1630.

GREENWICH CHAMBER OF COMMERCE. 175 Greenwich Avenue, Greenwich, CT 06830; (203) 869-3500.

Thimble Islands

Some of these islands are so tiny that a single house engulfs their rocky promontories.

Scattered across the waters of Long Island Sound, within five miles of the quaint little shoreline village of Stony Creek, lie the Lilliputian Thimble Islands. Some of these islands are so tiny that a single house engulfs their rocky promontories.

Named for the thimbleberry, a type of blackberry that once grew in profusion on the islands, they number well over three hundred. At last count — and at high tide — there were only about twenty-five inhabitable ones, and they range in size from less than a quarter of an acre to almost twenty acres. About 125 families summer here, some singly on an island and others in groups, with each family having its own small cottage. Many of these families have been coming back for generations — as many as seven generations in at least one case. At present all the islands are privately owned, and there is no public access, not even by private boat.

The Indians — Mettabeesecks, Mohegans, Narragansetts, and Pequots — were the first to spend their summers here, fishing and hunting. They particularly liked the superior granite found on the islands for making tools and weapons. So

The lone house on Belden Island, one of the Thimbles, receives its power from its own windmill, imported from Australia.

abundant was their production, in fact, that island gardeners today occasionally turn up artifacts.

Sheep-grazing pastures and rich oyster beds attracted the early colonists to the islands. The settlers also established a thriving shipbuilding industry on the islands of **East and West Crib** (about a mile from shore) that flourished for nearly one hundred fifty years. These two islands were named for their natural rock formations, which provided crude dry docks (or "cribs") for the builders.

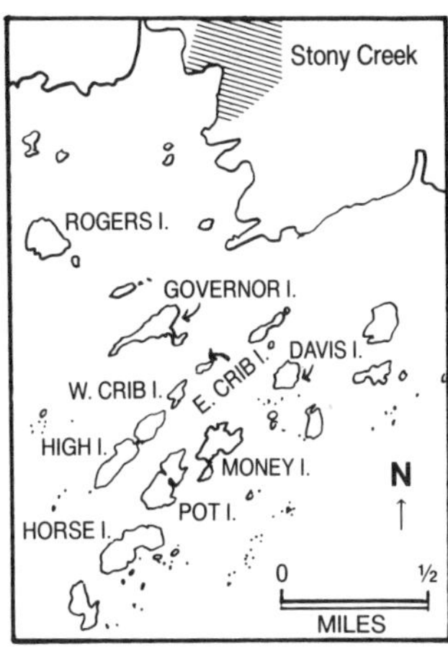

The Thimble Islands

Quarrying also became a major industry on the islands (and continues today in Stony Creek). The same pink granite that the Indians employed in making their tools and weapons was used in such illustrious monuments as the Statue of Liberty (for the statue's base), Grant's Tomb, and the Lincoln Memorial. (An interesting mainland side trip while visiting the Thimbles is to the **Stony Creek Quarry Preserve,** where hiking trails will lead you through parts of the quarry area.)

By 1870, the Thimbles had blossomed into a fashionable summer resort, actually being called, at this point, "The Newport of Connecticut." Gracious Victorian-style summer cottages, dripping with ornate gingerbread, were built, attracting wealthy and important visitors from around the country. (President William Howard Taft became so enthralled with the islands while a student at nearby Yale University that he decided to make the Summer White House there, on Davis Island, in 1910.) Hotels and guesthouses sprang up, offering such amenities as tennis courts, a six-hole golf course, and the first bowling alley built in the United States. Steamers carrying as many as two thousand passengers a day came from New Haven and New York to the islands, where their passengers swam, picnicked, played sports, and danced away the evening.

By 1870, the Thimbles had blossomed into a fashionable summer resort, actually being called, at this point, "The Newport of Connecticut."

The Great Depression and the 1938 "killer" hurricane put an end to all this gaiety, as many of the establishments on the island were washed away, never to be rebuilt. Some, of course, are still standing, and it is their antique charm that now enchants the visitor.

Probably nothing delights and captures the imaginations of young and old visitors alike, however, as does the lore of the infamous Captain Kidd and his buried treasure, particularly as it is shared by Captain Dwight Carter aboard the ***Volsunga III.*** Carter, his theatrical voice rising and falling with the dramatic events of his story, tells of Kidd, who hid from the British navy on High Island in the late

1600s and, legend has it, buried his fabulous treasure there. "But you know," says Carter in a raspy whisper, "down through the years ever since, we have dug this island up from one end to the other so many times I get an ache in my sacroiliac just telling you about it — and we haven't found any treasure yet. But we won't give up!"

The islanders who now live on **High Island** (it's the highest island, affording Captain Kidd's men a commanding view of the surrounding sea) call themselves the Buccaneers. All their houses and boats are painted black, and the Jolly Roger can often be seen flying from their flagpoles.

GRETCHEN MCFARLANE

Captain Dwight Carter spins tales of buried treasures and abandoned mothers-in-law on board his Volsunga III.

There are many more stories of the islands, not quite as sensational as that of Captain Kidd but no less vivid as told by Captain Carter. Particularly interesting are the tales of how many of the islands got their names. **Mother-In-Law** got its name, according to Carter, "when a young couple were married in the chapel on Money Island and decided to spend their honeymoon across the way on a barren rocky island. They rowed their boat and supplies over there. The bride's mother, however, decided to join them, so that night they gave her a good deal of wine with her dinner, and when she was asleep they took both boats and rowed back to Money Island, leaving the mother-in-law stranded for several days. To this day," Carter says with a mischievous chuckle, "that rock over there that now has a house on it is called Mother-In-Law Island."

Horse Island, the largest of the Thimbles, is now owned by Yale University and is used for ecological and marine biological research projects. According to Carter, a shipload of horses was wrecked off the reefs, and some of the horses swam to this island and lived there as wild horses for many years, thus giving the island its name. **Lantern Island** was appropriately named as a result of lighted lanterns being placed on the island during the quarrying days to guide schooners in and out of the harbor. "I don't have to make the stories up," Carter says, "they happen all the time out here."

A favorite, if questionable, yarn details the origin of the name **Pot Island.** It seems that at one time, around 1880, a men's club on the island used the island's glacially formed kettle-shaped potholes for an unusual drinking rite. The story goes that they filled a thirty-foot-deep pothole (sometimes called "Captain's Punch Bowl") with their tasty punch and did not leave the island until the hole had been completely drained, thus giving rise to the term "potted" and the name Pot Island. Such is the colorful legend and lore of the Thimbles!

Although the Thimble Islands themselves do not have public access, the dock area of the little village of **Stony Creek** is a great place for a stroll. It has several shops (crafts, antiques), two grocery stores with take-out and counter service, **Black-Eyed Susan's** coffee shop and seafood patio for breakfast and seafood, and **Bett's Marine,** where you can rent a rowboat for your own water tour of the islands or a little trolling.

Another way to see the islands is aboard the *J.N. Carter,* a sixty-six-foot sailing research vessel operated by **Schooner Inc.,** which leaves from the dock in New Haven. Schooner Inc., affiliated with Southern Connecticut State University and the New Haven Board of Education, has an ongoing marine biology research program that offers a series of educational trips around the islands for groups and individuals. For a membership fee of fifteen dollars you will receive a schedule of these trips, which are free to members. The trips (anywhere from a half-day to five days long) are part of Schooner Inc.'s regular research program, and passengers take part in activities such as collecting water samples, trolling for marine life, measuring fungi, and observing and taking notes of ecological changes.

The islanders who now live on High Island call themselves the Buccaneers. All their houses and boats are painted black, and the Jolly Roger can often be seen flying from their flagpoles.

Several moderately priced motels are located near the Branford-Stony Creek exit of I-95.

ACCESS

STONY CREEK. Directions: Take I-95 (Connecticut Turnpike) to exit 56, then follow signs to Stony Creek.

***VOLSUNGA III.* Directions:** From exit 56 of I-95 follow signs to Stony Creek, then take Leet's Island Road and Thimble Island Road to the town dock. **Season:** May through Columbus Day, hourly departures daily (trip takes 45 to 55 minutes). **Admission:** Charged. **Telephone:** (203) 481-3345. Parking is permitted along the main street (Thimble Island Road), and you can almost always find a space within easy walking distance. Also leaving from the Stony Creek town dock is the *SEA MIST,* captained by Mike Infantino. **Season:** Memorial Day through Columbus Day. **Admission:** Charged. **Telephone:** (203) 481-4841.

SCHOONER INC. For information regarding scheduled seasonal (mid-April to the end of October) trips, write to the organization at 60 South Water Street, New Haven, CT 06519, or call (203) 865-1737.

BRANFORD CHAMBER OF COMMERCE. 209 Montowese Street, Branford, CT 06405; (203) 488-5500.

RHODE ISLAND

The Jamestown Windmill, which operated from 1789 to 1896, has been fully restored and is now open to the public.

Most people know that Rhode Island is the smallest state in the Union, but few realize it also has the longest name, The State of Rhode Island and Providence Plantations. When you start talking "island" in this state, names can really get confusing. For instance, the largest island in the state is actually named Rhode Island, but it is also called Aquidneck Island. Although there are three towns on Aquidneck, one has gained such international fame that the whole island often is called by its name, Newport. The same confusion arises over the name of the island of Conanicut. Everyone calls it by the name of its one and only town, Jamestown.

Few, however, find cause for confusion with

Rhode Island's nickname, "the Ocean State." Not only is one-fifth of the state's 1,214-square-mile area covered by water (lakes, rivers, and bays), but Rhode Island also has four hundred miles of shoreline. Most of that shoreline surrounds the beautiful Narragansett Bay and its three major islands, Aquidneck, Conanicut, and Prudence. Another large island, Block, lies nine miles off Point Judith, which is located at the tip of the bay. Scattered about the bay are at least thirty additional tiny islands, most of them privately owned, wildlife preserves, or uninhabitable.

The ocean, the bay, and the large rivers of Rhode Island have played a leading role in shaping the development of the state. Some of the earliest settlements in the country were established on its islands, and Narragansett Bay has a long and impressive military history dating back to the Revolutionary War. History buffs will run out of time before seeing all the historical sites on these islands, many of which hold the distinction of being National Historic Landmarks.

The old saying "big things come in small packages" applies to this state. When it comes to seashore recreational facilities, Rhode Island is considered by most sporting enthusiasts to top the list in New England. It offers miles of sandy beaches and some of the best fishing in the country (year-round); just mention sailing and boating and you'll be told that you're in the "Yachting Capital of the World." Although the latter image was tarnished slightly in 1983 when the United States lost the *America*'s Cup race to Australia (the first time the U.S. had lost the cup in the race's 132-year history), the waters off the coast of Newport are seething with challengers bent on bringing the cup back "home."

There's much to see and do in Rhode Island, and none of it will disappoint you.

Block Island

It may well be true that "a rose by any other name would smell as sweet," but one still wishes the settlers of Block Island had stuck to one of the island's earlier names. Manisses, as the Indians called it, and Claudia, as it was designated by the Italian explorer Verrazano, and particularly Adriaen's Eylant, for Adriaen Block, the Dutch navigator who put the island on the map, all have a much classier ring to them and better personify this lovely Victorian idyll than the functional sounding "Block." Somehow Block just doesn't do justice to this gently rolling bit of landscape, dotted with glistening freshwater ponds, fruit orchards, and spectacular clay cliffs that tower almost two hundred feet above the miles of cream-colored beaches.

The fact that the shape of the island is almost always described as that of a pork chop does not do much to enhance the island's image either. Try, as some publicity person has, to liken the shape to that of a teardrop and it just doesn't click. It's definitely a pork chop! But from the shank to the loin — an area only seven miles at its longest and three miles at its widest points (barely eleven square miles of land) — it's all delicious.

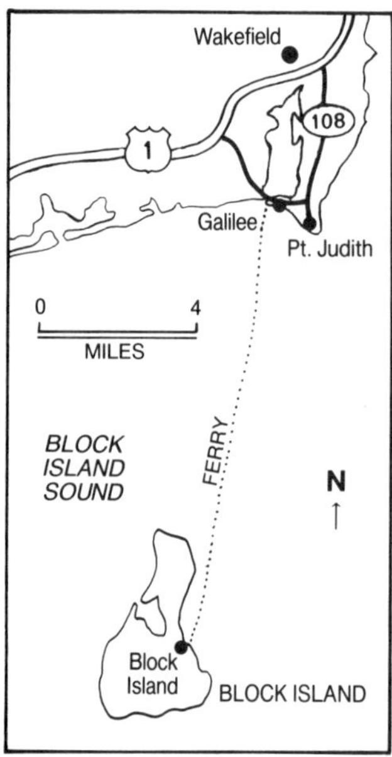

Block Island

The island's more than twenty miles of hardtop roads are ideal for biking. For hikers, its innumerable dirt roads meander through luscious thickets of honeysuckle, chicory, bayberry, Queen Anne's lace, and butter-and-eggs, as well as great patches of blackberries. Crisscrossing the island's small farms and meadowlands are the historic remains of stone walls — more than four hundred miles of them — delineating old land boundaries and behind which sheep and cattle were protected in this once-prosperous farming community.

As with so many other islands, the early history of "The Block" is one of Indians and British settlers using the land for farming and the shores and lakes for fishing. The treacherous rocks, shoals, and sandbars surrounding the island have, however, laden its history with fascinating stories of shipwrecks. When the *Spartan*, for example, broke up on the rocks in 1831, its huge cargo of cotton cloth was washed ashore. Gleefully, the island women stretched the bolts of cloth across a nearby hillside to dry, forever dubbing the area "Calico Hill." Similarly Cow Cove was named when another ship was wrecked, forcing its cargo of cattle to swim ashore.

While farming and fishing remain important parts of the island's economy, the Victorian tourist boom, sparked in the mid-nineteenth century and lasting through the early 1930s, left an indelible mark here. During its heyday at the turn of the century, Block Island was a fashionable summer resort for genteel Victorians. Never quite rivaling its fabled neighbor to the north, Newport, or that city's lavish summer homes, Block Island was more inclined toward large summer hotels with huge wraparound porches replete with wicker rockers and striped awnings. Leisurely parasol strolls, lawn cro-

JOHN VEDRAL

You may need to bring an overnight bag to have time to enjoy all the pleasures available on "The Block."

quet, and small garden teas highlighted the day's activity.

But as happened to so many other island resorts of the period, hurricanes and fires took their toll, and as the automobile made mainland resorts more accessible, Block Island fell into disuse and disrepair. For many years there was a kind of honky-tonk atmosphere in the village, with hoards of day-trippers, mostly college-age youths, coming over to picnic, drink beer, and swim. Since the 1960s, however, the island has seen a renaissance in tourism. Most of the once-decrepit hotels have been snapped up by entrepreneurs and restored to their Victorian splendor — fortunately, with modern plumbing.

The twelve-mile trip out from Galilee takes about an hour and ten minutes, and if you're at all inclined to sea sickness, check the ferry schedule carefully. A small and a large ferry operate alternately, and the larger of the two handles the often-turbulent sea with a minimum of discomfort.

Your first sight of the island is the Mohegan Bluffs, high, jagged cliffs that jut out into the open sea, somewhat resembling the cliffs of Gay Head on Martha's Vineyard and seriously eroding each year from the battering sea. As the ferry approaches the pier in Old Harbor, the village of New Shoreham, looking for all the world like a façade of an old Hollywood movie set, stretches out along the main street. Several enormous old hotels, most notably the newly restored **National Hotel,** dominate the skyline. Along with a cluster of shops, churches, restaurants, guesthouses, and other small buildings, a tangle of fishing, sightseeing, and pleasure boats fills the bustling harbor area.

Although Block Island appeals most to those

Leisurely parasol strolls, lawn croquet, and small garden teas highlighted the day's activity.

JOHN VEDRAL

Few sights say New England better than a low-lying stone wall.

who like their activities low-key and unstructured, there is plenty for everyone to do. All twenty-five miles of Block Island beaches belong to the public, and **Crescent Beach,** on the eastern shore, has lifeguards and a beach pavilion (snack bar), making it very popular for all beach activities. If you don't mind heights or a bit of a climb, a long series of wooden steps built out over the edge and sides of **Mohegan Bluffs** leads down to a spectacular beach where surfing, beachcombing, kite-flying, and, of course, swimming are the best. Children enjoy beachcombing and collecting rocks at **Pebbly Beach** near the ferry landing in Old Harbor. According to local history, the streets of many seaport towns in Connecticut and Rhode Island, including New London and Newport, were paved with small cobblestones and pebbles gathered from this beach.

The only evidence to support the island's motto, "The Bermuda of the North," is its constant parade of bikers. Biking is still the best way to get around here, and several bike and moped rental shops offer children's bikes, adult bikes (some with baby seats attached), and tandems. Many islanders are dead set against the use of mopeds on the island (you'll see bumper stickers reading "NOPEDS"), so be prepared for a few disgruntled comments if you choose to use one.

The island has some exceptional hiking areas, including **The Maze,** eleven miles of carefully cut paths that wind through heavenly scented pine forest and merge on the cliffs at the northeast end of the island. **Rodman's Hollow** is a treat for the naturalist, taking you on paths to a natural ravine and a wildlife sanctuary. This is a nice place to bring children for a picnic and exploring, as they are apt to catch sight of deer here. There is also a newly formed **Audubon Society trail system** along the edge of Dicken's Farm that you can travel alone or at scheduled times with a naturalist. Nesting areas of rare birds such as the grasshopper sparrow, marsh hawk, and upland plover can be sighted here. And in the fall you may well catch the spectacular flights of peregrine falcons. Because the island is strategically located on the Atlantic Flyway, some ornithologists say that it is the best spot in the Northeast for bird watching.

The **Block Island Historical Society** and the **Island Free Library** are open daily in the summer, and both contain interesting collections of information on the island's past. Many notorious pirates have been suspected of burying their booty on "The Block." Here are a few hot tips: Captain Kidd is said to have buried chests (of gold?) on the Old Road near Harbor School House; Samuel Ball, who lived on the island more than one hundred years ago and unearthed a kettle of gold, reburied it somewhere near the center of town; and more money (silver) is said to be buried near the old Litchfield house way out on Corn Neck Road. Don't forget your metal detector!

The fishing on Block Island is excellent. Surf-casting along all the beaches as well as from the town breakwater is very popular. If you never have tried your hand (or foot!) at quahauging, this is the place to do so. You do have to pay a fee for a nonresident's shellfish license, but be assured it's worth it. All fishing equipment, including tackle, bait, and rowboats, is available on the island at several shops.

A fairly wide assortment of accommodations is available on the island, from small, inexpensive guesthouses to sophisticated hotels. Most hotels require a minimum stay of two nights on weekends and give special rates for a mid-week, three-night stay. A few hotels, such as the **New Shoreham House Inn,** offer rooms with a cot or crib for children.

Because the island is strategically located on the Atlantic Flyway, some ornithologists say that it is the best spot in the Northeast for bird watching.

While fast-food chains and haute cuisine are lacking on the island, you can find just about everything in between. Many of the hotel dining rooms are open to the public (dinner reservations during the busy summer months are a must), and several grocery stores sell cookout and picnic supplies. Seafood — especially swordfish — is the island specialty, but you can order such entrées as chicken cacciatore, pizza, or filet mignon in many establishments. A few menu items have become local legends, for example the smiling-face pancakes at the **Surf Hotel,** lobster-in-the-rough at **Ballard's,** the Raw Bar at the **Hotel Manisses,** the "Blockbuster" (a potent rum drink) at **The 1661 Inn,** and almost anything at **The Cat 'n the Fiddle.**

Not everyone on Block Island likes to go to bed early, so the nightlife is active. There's jazz at **Captain Nick's,** several piano bars featuring country and western music, and rock music, dancing, and a stand-up comedian at Ballard's on the waterfront. There is even an old movie theater, **The Empire,** which features fairly recent movies that change about twice a week.

On rainy days you can visit the shops of **Old Harbor,** where you can browse or purchase island-made crafts, kites, books, gifts, or pastries. Near the shops you'll also find the wide front veranda of the National Hotel, where you can rock, sip, and watch the action. The National has a commanding view of the harbor, and its wonderful porch, where breakfast, lunch, and cocktails are served, acts as a magnet to guests and visitors throughout the day and into the evening. Remember to try a cup of homemade clam chowder at **Payne's** on the New Harbor dock or at **Dead Eye Dick's,** the island's oldest restaurant.

Antique collectors will find a particularly fine antique shop in the village (Old Harbor) called the **Manisses Attic Antique Shop.** It's run by the Abrams family, who are responsible for restoring two Block Island landmarks, The 1661 Inn and the Hotel Manisses. Both hotels are filled with authentic Victorian antiques collected by Justin Abrams, and what doesn't go into the hotels goes into the antique shop. This includes furniture, paintings, and other art objects — but nothing that is too big to be carted away on the ferry.

Kids are almost never disappointed in their attempts to get kites aloft.

The island also has several toy shops. **Christopher Ryan International Toys** offers only "child-tested" toys (tested by the owner's two sons), including a great selection from around the world — Lego, Hasbro, Steiff, Hi-Flyes, Dakin, and the like. **Airborne Kites** and **The Kite Store** are not only colorful and interesting shops to visit, but they are always busy. You can usually depend on a good wind on Block Island, so kite-flying is a popular sport for the novice or the expert. Kids are almost never disappointed in their attempts to get kites aloft, and some of the more amazing stunt kites and one-of-a-kind collector's items (sold at Airborne) are fun to watch.

ACCESS

POINT JUDITH (GALILEE). Directions: From I-95 south take exit 92 (North Stonington – Westerly), bearing right onto North Stonington Road. Continue until Westerly bypass. Take right bypass (Route 78) to the end, then turn left onto Route 1. Follow Route 1 to the exit for Route 108 (Galilee). Bear right off the exit to Point Judith Road and follow Point Judith Road to the dock for the Block Island Ferry (on your left). From I-95 north take Route 4 to Route 1, then proceed as above.

INTERSTATE NAVIGATION COMPANY. Point Judith is the main point of embarkation for Block Island, but during the summer months ferries also leave Providence and Newport, Rhode Island, and New London, Connecticut. Parking available (fee). **Season:** Year-round from Point Judith; late June to early September from Providence, Newport, and New London. **Admission:** Charged. **Telephone:** (401) 783-4613; for New London call (203) 442-7891. **Note:** The ferry sometimes lands in New Harbor. Directions provided here are from the ferry landing in Old Harbor.

JOHN VEDRAL

For the nature lover, a walk along the trail through Rodman's Hollow is a must.

NEW ENGLAND AIRLINES. Flights from 6 A.M. through 8:30 P.M. from Westerly, Rhode Island, to Block Island are scheduled daily. **Season:** Year-round. **Admission:** Charged (children half fare). **Telephone:** (401) 596-2460. Taxi service on Block Island is plentiful and available at the airport as well as the ferry landing.

BLOCK ISLAND HISTORICAL SOCIETY. Directions: From the ferry landing follow Water Street a short distance to Dodge Street to the corner of Ocean Avenue. The museum is on the corner opposite the post office. **Season:** June through mid-September. **Admission:** Free.

ISLAND FREE LIBRARY. Directions: Located on Dodge Street just around the corner from the National Hotel. **Season:** Year-round. **Admission:** Free. **Telephone:** (401) 466-5970.

MANISSES ATTIC ANTIQUE SHOP. Directions: From the ferry landing follow Water Street to the left, and the shop is at the intersection (Rebecca's statue) on your left. **Season:** May to October. **Telephone:** (401) 466-2421.

CHRISTOPHER RYAN INTERNATIONAL TOYS. Directions: From the ferry landing go left on Water Street (near the theater). **Season:** June through September.

AIRBORNE KITES. Directions: Located on Dodge Street, just off Water Street. **Season:** June through September.

THE KITE STORE. Directions: Walk up Dodge Street (from Water Street) and turn right onto Corn Neck Road. The shop is a few doors down on the right. **Season:** June through September.

BLOCK ISLAND CHAMBER OF COMMERCE. Drawer D, Block Island, RI 02807; (401) 466-2982.

Conanicut (Jamestown)

Island hopping began on Conanicut Island. This small island, nine miles long and about a mile wide, located at the mouth of Narragansett Bay, was the site of the first ferry system in the country. Because all the earliest settlements in Rhode Island were established on islands, the ferry system connecting one island to another and the islands to the mainland provided a vital link among all the inhabitants of the area. The bay was the "highway" connecting the original settlements, and the ferries were the transportation system. In fact, many historical overviews of Rhode Island begin by mentioning that Roger Williams, the founder of the state, arrived in what is now Providence in a dugout canoe in 1636.

This island was called Conanicut by the Narragansett Indians in honor of their sachem (chief), Conanicus. In 1656 a group of English defectors from the Massachusetts Bay Colony led by Benedict Arnold (great-grandfather of the traitor) purchased Conanicut from the Indians, retained the name, and called their first settlement Jamestown in honor of King James II of England. Because the Jamestown ferry became so important over the years (the ferry was replaced by the Jamestown Bridge in 1940), and also because the small village of Jamestown has remained the only center of activity here, the island is often referred to by that name.

Caroline Head is a volunteer at the Jamestown Museum.

The **Jamestown Museum**, located in a nineteenth-century schoolhouse in the center of town, features hands-on exhibits and memorabilia that illustrate various aspects of the island's history. (Exhibits change annually.) A permanent exhibit displays memorabilia from the early ferry system, which operated for more than three hundred years. Ferries were the first public utilities regulated by the colonial government, and rules and regulations governing them were quite exact. The ferryman was required, for instance, to transport "Physicians, Surgeons, or Midwives, at any Time of Night," and on Sundays he was required to transport passengers to and from places of worship. Of the seventy-five ferries that operated within the state of Rhode Island from 1640 to 1940, at least one-third of them had a landing in Jamestown.

The first regulated ferries, operating during the late 1600s, were sailboats made of heavy timbers and were about thirty-five feet long and fourteen feet wide. They carried animals as well as humans,

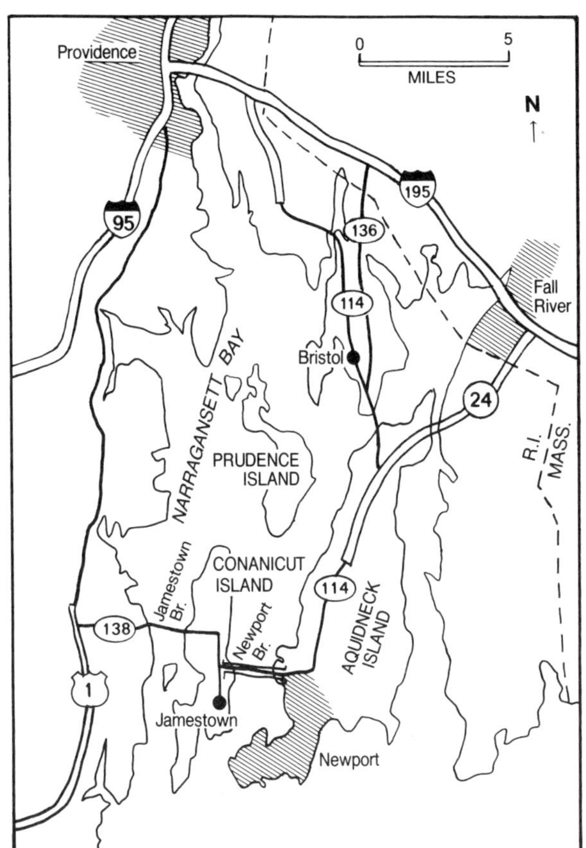

Conanicut, Aquidneck, and Prudence Islands

and when they were beset by calms, the boat ride across the bay was anything but pleasant. The length of a trip might unexpectedly extend to hours, sometimes overnight, and the noise and stench from the animals could be overwhelming. The horse ferry was the next method of crossing the waterways, and while it overcame the becalming difficulties, it produced other problems. The horse ferry was a boat with paddle wheels on each side connected to a shaft that was geared to a treadmill. A pair of horses worked the treadmill, setting the paddle wheels in motion. If the seas were the slightest bit rough, however, the horses would lose their footing and continually slip off the treadmill. Consequently, the horse ferry was short-lived, and passengers were happy to see the invention of "steamers."

This small island, nine miles long and about a mile wide, located at the mouth of Narragansett Bay, was the site of the first ferry system in the country.

The steam ferries crossed the West Passage of Narragansett Bay from the mainland to Jamestown until the Jamestown Bridge was built in 1940. Another ferry crossed the East Passage from Jamestown to Newport until the Newport Bridge was completed in 1969. This ancient route across Narragansett Bay through Conanicut Island (now Route 138) has been called "the oldest transportation route in America."

Since the opening of the two bridges, most traffic simply scurries over Route 138, which cuts across Conanicut, ignoring most of what Jamestown has to offer. The roads from the center of town lead toward verdant farmland to the north, passing some early houses and an old windmill, while to the south the road winds past antique forts that once guarded the entrance to Narragansett Bay. The rich, earthy smell of farmland mingles with fresh salt air at every bend in the lightly traveled roads, and you experience a general feeling of stepping back in time on Conanicut.

The village area of Jamestown, bordering the island's east shore and facing Newport, has seen a recent trend toward modernization. In spite of this, many vestiges of a bygone era linger. An old ferryboat at the once-bustling East Ferry Landing, unsuccessfully resurrected as a hotel/restaurant, rusts away at its mooring. While new condominiums now occupy the nearby site of the old Bay View Hotel, just down the main street a semicircle of century-old, gray-shingled summer homes skirts the scenic harbor. And anchored at the other end of the harbor, almost in the shadow of the Newport Bridge (spanning the east channel between Conanicut and Aquidneck), is another century-old dwelling, **The Bay Voyage Hotel.** This building, newly renovated into a time-sharing facility, is aptly named. It was once located across the bay in Newport, but in 1889 an entrepreneur, thinking Jamestown offered more potential for tourism than Newport, had it floated across the bay.

Watson Farm out on North Road is a two-hundred-eighty-acre working farm that is open to the public all summer and fall. The property is complete with walking paths and orchards as well as herds of sheep, Black Angus cattle, horses, and other farm animals that children enjoy seeing close up. Just down the road from the farm is the **Jamestown Windmill,** which operated from 1789 to 1896 and is now fully restored. It is open for inspection and guided tours during the summer months.

At the southernmost tip of the island is **Beaver Tail Lighthouse**, first established in 1749. The original structure was burned by the British in 1779, but the foundation, an interesting example of early

Beaver Tail Lighthouse has been a landmark at the entrance to Narragansett Bay since 1749.

JIM DANIELS/PROVIDENCE JOURNAL

Scuba divers find the coves of Fort Wetherill State Park ideal for the pursuit of their hobby.

colonial stonework, remains. The present lighthouse dates from 1856 and has been used for the development of different types of foghorns. Surrounding the lighthouse is a broad shelf of layered rocks that, during low tide, provides a wonderful area for climbing, surfcasting, kite-flying, and picnicking. When the tide is high, and particularly when the sea is heavy, the crashing of waves over these rocks is awesome.

Three forts and many other recreational activities are located on the island. **Fort Wetherill State Park** contains huge remnants of the old fort, including steps leading up to ramparts from which you enjoy commanding views of the entire bay. Several small coves in the park are perfect for snorkeling and scuba diving. According to the **Audubon Society of Rhode Island,** which makes special guided trips to Jamestown, "the waters off Fort Wetherill have the reputation among divers of having the best visibility in the area." Audubon expedition leaders instruct groups in basic snorkeling techniques. **Jamestown Scuba** (in downtown) also provides lessons and rents and sells equipment. On most summer weekends you can watch divers taking lessons or exploring these coves.

"The waters off Fort Wetherill have the reputation among divers of having the best visibility in the area."

The roads on Jamestown are gently rolling or flat and are lightly traveled, so biking is an excellent way of getting around. All the recreational areas are within easy biking distance of the center of town. There is a fairly large beach for swimming at **Mackerel Cove** and smaller ones at Fort Wetherill and **Fort Getty.** Fort Getty also is a popular spot for camping, picnicking, fishing, and boating.

Two other small museums join the Jamestown Museum in the center of town: the **Sydney L. Wright Museum** in the Jamestown Philomenian Library displays Indian artifacts from prehistoric times through the early colonial period, and the **Fire Museum** exhibits some of the early fire-fighting equipment used in Jamestown, including a horse-drawn pumper.

Accommodations on the island are quite limited, but there are a few bed and breakfast guesthouses and a small motel on Route 138. In the center of town and surrounding the harbor are several small shops and restaurants. **Pal's Treat Shop** on Ferry Wharf has excellent ice cream, and **Fuzzy's** on Narragansett Avenue serves very good Italian food and prepares sandwiches for take-out.

ACCESS

CONANICUT ISLAND (JAMESTOWN). Directions: Routes 1 and Scenic 1A both intersect Route 138. Take Route 138 east, following signs to the Jamestown Bridge. Turn right onto North Road and follow it to the center of Jamestown and the harbor area.

THE JAMESTOWN MUSEUM. Directions: From Route 138 take North Main Road south. Turn left onto Narragansett Avenue. The museum is on the left side of the street. **Season:** Mid-June through August. **Admission:** Free. **Telephone:** (401) 423-0784.

WATSON FARM. Directions: From Route 138 take North Main Road south. The Watson Farm is on your right. **Season:** June 1 through October 15. **Admission:** Free. **Telephone:** (401) 423-0005.

FORT WETHERILL STATE PARK. Directions: From Route 138 travel south on North Main Road, through Jamestown center (road becomes Southwest Avenue). Turn left onto Highland Road. At the next traffic circle (about 1½ miles) signs to Fort Wetherill are just ahead on your right. **Season:** Year-round. **Admission:** Free.

AUDUBON SOCIETY OF RHODE ISLAND (GREAT EXPEDITIONS). Write to Great Expeditions Field Trip Program, Audubon Society of Rhode Island, 40 Bowen Street, Providence, RI 02903, or call (401) 521-1670.

JAMESTOWN SCUBA. Directions: From Route 138 follow North Main Road south to Narragansett Avenue. Turn left, and the scuba shop is on your right. **Season:** Year-round. **Telephone:** (401) 423-1662.

JAMESTOWN TOWN CLERK'S OFFICE. For further information regarding hunting and fishing regulations, accommodations, etc., write to 93 Narragansett Avenue, Jamestown, RI 02835, or call (401) 423-0200.

A couple of would-be skippers investigate the docks at Newport.

Aquidneck Island (Newport)

The Narragansett Indians, the first people to settle here, named the island Aquidneck, meaning "Isle of Peace." In 1524 the Italian explorer Verrazano was so impressed with the profusion of wild roses growing along its shores that he named it Rhode Island after the Greek island of Rhodes. But to the millions of tourists who cross one of the three bridges connecting it to the mainland, and particularly to the thousands of sailors who sail up the sparkling blue waters of Narragansett Bay each summer, it is Newport.

Newport. The very name conjures up a wealth of images from America's Gilded Age: marble palaces with golden rooms, crystal chandeliers, sweeping lime-green lawns rolling down to the sea, and the wealthiest of the wealthy Americans bedecked in their jewel-encrusted finery, dining on sumptuous feasts in their grand mansions.

The Narragansett Indians, the first people to settle here, named the island Aquidneck, meaning "Isle of Peace."

Although there is much more to see and do in Newport than tour the many splendid **mansions**, these are still the major attraction. People still live in many of the huge homes, which you can see from **Cliff Walk,** a three-mile hike that skirts the ocean and the front lawns of the "cottages," as the homes are called. Seven of the most magnificent, however, are now owned by the Preservation Society of Newport County, while others, although privately owned, are also open to the public for tours. Most of these mansions are located along Bellevue Avenue, a short walk from the center of town. The privately

Beechwood, once the home of "The Mrs. Astor," is one of several Newport mansions open to visitors.

owned **Beechwood** was the home of Caroline Astor (or "The Mrs. Astor," as she preferred to be called), the undisputed queen of Newport society throughout most of its Gilded Age.

While some of the other mansions, such as **The Breakers, Marble House,** and **The Elms**, are considerably more ornate, there is a limit to one's ability to travel amid such grandeur, and Beechwood, with its understated elegance (for that period), is a good place to start.

What is particularly fun and interesting about Beechwood is that throughout your visit — from your entry at the gate, where you are handed your "calling card" by the butler, to your spot of Mrs. Astor's famous strawberry tea in the kitchen just before departing — you are welcomed as a personal guest of Mrs. Astor. You never get to see her, of course (except for the larger-than-life portrait in the front reception hall), but you are treated to a tour of the mansion by her extremely personable staff, and you get to meet several other house guests along the way.

Rosecliff, built in 1902 by the renowned architect Stanford White and modeled after the Grand Trianon at Versailles, is one of the more popular mansions among tourists. It was the backdrop for many of the scenes from the 1974 movie version of *The Great Gatsby*, which highlighted another important (and much later) era of Newport society.

Lately, the stately mansions of Newport — many of which are open on weekends throughout the year — have become more than just settings for fanciful re-enactments of the Gilded Age. Increasingly they are being rented out for everything "from a simple, elegant dinner party to as lavish as you want to get," as Linda Naiss, director of Beechwood Services, Inc., puts it. Still, the first priority at Beechwood, says Naiss, "is to retain the feeling here of a gracious home." Be sure to drop by Beechwood, if only for a cup of that delicious strawberry tea.

Aquidneck, which is fifteen miles long and five miles wide, has three towns, Newport, Middletown, and Portsmouth. It was purchased from the Narragansett Indians in 1636 by early followers of Roger Williams. Williams, who was banished from the Massachusetts Bay Colony for his liberal religious beliefs, had already established the first settlement in this area, calling it Providence. The exiled Puritans who came to Aquidneck were led by Anne Hutchinson and settled in Portsmouth. Another group moved on to settle Newport. Because of Williams's guarantee of complete religious freedom to anyone who settled in Rhode Island, various religious groups, including Jews and Quakers, were attracted to this area.

If you take one of the many walking tours through the historic district of Newport, you will find the oldest Jewish house of worship in North America, the **Touro Synagogue**, built in 1763, and the **Quaker Meeting House**, built in 1699. There are many early Newport homes and establishments to visit as well, including the **Wanton-Lyman-Hazard House**, circa 1675, and the **White Horse Tavern**, the oldest operating tavern in America, built around 1673 and still offering a fine bill of fare.

Almost any side street you wander will provide some charming discovery.

Bowen's Wharf and **Banister's Wharf,** their cobblestones dating from the eighteenth century, now support myriad small shops, restaurants, and craft workshops. **Brick Market Place,** a National Historic Landmark, was once Newport's town hall and now is a showcase for original art, Newport prints, and gifts.

Thames Street is one of the busiest shopping and browsing areas, but almost any side street you wander will provide some charming discovery. **Lily's of the Alley**, a short distance up Spring Street from the center of town, run by Maggie Philbrick and Janet Skinner, is a potpourri of imported cotton clothing at very reasonable prices. Lily's also has shelves full of wonderfully scented soaps, oils, and body lotions.

Rue de France on lower Thames Street is an inviting little shop. Pamela Kelley, the proprietor, fell in love with the lace curtains she found all over Marais, the oldest section of Paris, while she and her husband were living there. After investigating and finding out where they were made, the couple decided to import the lace to America. They opened their shop a few years ago and have a thriving mail-order business in custom-made curtains, pillow covers, bed ruffles, and canopies.

A great shop to visit — which is as much a museum as it is a retail store — is the **Army and Navy Surplus Store** on Thames Street. It's one of the original such stores and the kind of place where you want to try on everything just for the heck of it. Richie Blackman, one of the owners, is good-natured about sightseers prowling through his gear, which is not surprising since he has everyone from the "Newport 400" to Canadian fishermen as steady customers. Vietnam jungle combat boots have been one of the big sellers recently, along with high-top

Richie Blackman runs the Army and Navy Surplus Store that is part retail outlet, part museum.

sneakers. The latter come in basic gray, white, black, and camouflage as well as shocking pink and gold lamé (up to size 15).

You'd probably have a hard time naming one sport that isn't played at some level on Aquidneck. American lawn tennis began here at the **Newport Casino** more than one hundred years ago, and the only grass courts open to the public in this country are right here at the casino. This vintage landmark, built in 1880 and designed by Stanford White, also houses the **International Tennis Hall of Fame and Museum.**

Glen Farm in Portsmouth is the scene of many exciting polo matches (bring your own blanket and box lunch — admission is free) as well as the International Jumping Derby every August. One of the few frontons for jai alai (originated by the Basques and said to be the fastest game in the world) is the Newport Jai Alai Sports Theater in Middletown.

Fishing charters are available year-round, and ice fishing is very popular on the many ponds in the area. The **Norman Bird Sanctuary**, which has an interesting program of activities throughout the year (special programs for children), is also a popular spot for cross-country skiing in the winter.

On weekends from May through September there is usually a boat show taking place at the **Newport Yachting Center** in downtown Newport. International boat races often take place as well. Two particularly good spots from which to watch these races are the lively **Inn at Castle Hill** and the more sedate **Oceancliff Resort**. Both provide drinks, light snacks, and full-course dinners, and both are located on **Ocean Drive.** On almost any spot along this scenic road, you'll find plenty of beaches and low rocky places for fishing, snorkeling, swimming, rock climbing, Frisbee playing, and just about any other outdoor activity.

Music festivals have always been a big addition to the summer scene in Newport. Outstanding musicians and singers from around the world, some making their American debut, often perform in the classic setting of the music room or outdoor terrace of a Bellevue Avenue mansion. Folk and jazz festivals are held in the summer, and other concerts are sponsored year-round.

Outstanding musicians and singers from around the world, some making their American debut, often perform in the classic setting of the music room or outdoor terrace of a Bellevue Avenue mansion.

Many tours of the island are available by bus, trolley, taxi, and boat. The free **Newport Loop bus** makes twenty-seven stops throughout the city. This bus runs only in the summer, but public transportation is available on the island throughout the year.

The local airport in Middletown serves only private and charter planes (Watch Hill Airlines and Coastal Airlines), but a frequent taxi shuttle (Cozy Cab) goes to Theodore Francis Green State Airport in Warwick.

Many of Aquidneck's hotels, restaurants, guesthouses, shops, and sightseeing attractions are open throughout the year. **Christmas-in-Newport** is a month-long program of Christmas events held in different locations throughout the county, including the Christmas Tree Lighting at the Newport Yachting Center and the Annual Christmas Craft and Marketplace on Goat Island (connected by a short causeway to Newport).

One of the island's most unusual — and most delightful — spots is Portsmouth's **Green Animals** topiary gardens. These whimsical gardens, filled with plants shaped into animal forms, are among the best topiary gardens in the country. They were started by Thomas Brayton about 1880 and are arranged around the formal gardens of his former estate. Children will have fun picking out their favorites among the eighty shapes. A garden shop offers herbs and plants for sale, and there is a children's Victorian toy museum to visit. The museum is located in the former home of the Brayton family, just inside the entrance to the grounds.

Gardener Tom Shiekey gives Frankenstein a trim at Portsmouth's Green Animals topiary gardens.

ACCESS

AQUIDNECK ISLAND. Directions: *(From Providence, Rhode Island)* Take I-195 east to exit 2, Route 136 south. Cross the Mt. Hope Bridge (toll) and follow Route 114 south to Portsmouth, Middletown, and Newport. The visitor's center in Newport is located on America's Cup Avenue. *(From points south and west)* Take Route 1 to Route 138 in Kingston, Rhode Island. Cross the Jamestown and the Newport bridges (toll). Turn right off the bridge to downtown Newport and America's Cup Avenue. *(From Fall River, Massachusetts)* Take Route 24 south, crossing the bridge at Tiverton. Route 24 becomes Route 114 in Portsmouth.

NEWPORT MANSIONS. Directions: Drive south on America's Cup Avenue from downtown Newport. Turn left onto Memorial Boulevard, then take the second right, which is Bellevue Avenue (most of the mansions are along here). **Season:** Year-round. **Admission:** Charged. **Telephone (Preservation Society of Newport County):** (401) 847-1000; **(Beechwood)** (401) 846-3772.

LILY'S OF THE ALLEY: Directions: From the Pedestrian Walk in downtown Newport walk up Touro Street to the corner of Spring Street. Lily's is number 64 Spring Street. **Season:** Year-round. **Telephone:** (401) 846-7545.

RUE DE FRANCE. Directions: Walking north from downtown on Thames Street, the store is on your right. **Season:** Year-round. **Telephone:** (401) 846-2084.

ARMY AND NAVY SURPLUS STORE. Directions: At 262 Thames Street, across from Banister's Wharf in downtown Newport. **Season:** Year-round. **Telephone:** (401) 847-3073.

GLEN FARM (Portsmouth). Directions: From the Mt. Hope Bridge or Tiverton Bridge take Route 138 south. The farm is about five miles toward Newport on your left. **Season:** Year-round. **Admission:** Polo matches are free; for other events there is a charge. **Telephone:** (401) 847-4490. **Newport Polo Association:** (401) 846-0442.

NORMAN BIRD SANCTUARY (Middletown). Directions: From Route 114 or Route 138 follow Green End Avenue east to Third Beach Road, which passes the sanctuary. **Season:** Year-round. **Admission:** Charged. **Telephone:** (401) 846-2577.

GREEN ANIMALS (Portsmouth). Directions: After crossing the Mt. Hope Bridge, follow Route 114 south for about three miles to Cory's Lane. Turn right onto Cory's Lane, and the gardens are a short distance down the road. **Season:** May 1 to September 30, and Sundays and holidays in October. **Admission:** Charged. **Telephone (The Preservation Society of Newport County):** (401) 847-1000.

Prudence Island

According to the author of the only history book written about the island, most Rhode Islanders "don't even know where Prudence Island is located."

This little island, seven miles in length and slightly more than a mile across at its widest, truly deserves its nickname, "The Whale in the Bay." Its comical shape closely resembles that of a whale — complete with flippers!

The island, which lies in the center of Narragansett Bay, originally was called Chibachuwese (chi-ba-CHU-wese) by the Indians, which loosely translated means "separation of the passage." When it was purchased from the Indians in about 1637 by the founder of Rhode Island, Roger Williams, he changed the name to Prudence.

According to the author of the only history book written about the island (actually a chronology of facts), most Rhode Islanders "don't even know where Prudence Island is located, and quite a number have never even heard of it." To the majority of Prudence Island inhabitants that's perfectly fine. They would just as soon keep this wonderful little secret to themselves. Ask an islander about bringing your car to the island, and the response is

RI DEPT. OF ENVIRONMENTAL MANAGEMENT

Indians originally called Prudence Island Chibachuwese, which can be loosely translated as "separation of the passage."

likely to be: "What would you want to do that for? There isn't any place to drive to." Or ask an equally stupid question, "What do you do on Prudence Island?" and you can expect an emphatic "Absolutely *nothing!*"

The island lies approximately four miles out from the historic town of Bristol and is only a thirty-minute ferry ride away. The ferry stops at two docks, **Homestead,** where one of the island stores is located, and **Sandy Point.**

It's an easy mile walk along Narragansett Avenue, which hugs the coast from Sandy Point to Homestead, so you can get off at either stop. Along the way you'll pass a row of neat little cottages with flower-filled gardens and window boxes, the Union Church, a minuscule post office, and several dead-end roads, one of which (well-marked) leads to the island's gift shop, **The Anchorage.**

Just up the hill from Sandy Point is a main road with the incongruous name of **Broadway,** which crosses the island at its widest point. Along it is the island's one-room schoolhouse, which until recently had been in continuous operation since 1896. Improved ferry service now makes it possible for island children to attend school on the mainland.

Heritage Foundation, also along Broadway, provides a mile-long nature walk through a thickly forested area inhabited by a large number of deer. The island is said to have more deer per acre than any other spot in New England. Along with deer, however, the island has a large population of *Ixodes dammini* ticks, which can cause serious illness. If you're walking through the woods, that's something you want to watch out for.

The island is said to have more deer per acre than any other spot in New England.

The **Prudence Inn,** which provides the only public overnight accommodations on the island, is located just a short walk from Sandy Point. The inn offers the following: a bed and breakfast plan; special "weekender" packages, which include a walking tour of the island conducted by a member of the staff; and a limited number of two- and three-bedroom cottages for rent by the week from mid-May to mid-October. The inn also has the only restaurant on the island — and it is a good one at that. There are, however, two stores, **Marcy's** and **Deano's,** where you can buy the makings of a picnic lunch.

While the middle portion of the island is privately owned (there's a large vineyard and winery here, producing Prudence Island wine), more than thirteen hundred acres of park land have been established on the island's northern and southern ends. All of this acreage is part of the **Bay Islands Park,** a twenty-six-hundred-acre recreational area stretching from Conanicut Island at the southern end of Narragansett Bay to Patience Island just off the northern tip of Prudence.

The summer ferries from Providence and Portsmouth visit **South Prudence Park**, which serves as the center for the Bay Islands Park, where visitors can picnic, fish, camp, and explore the island's pine forests, cranberry bogs, and rocky shores. Ten miles of trails offer hikers the opportunity to explore on their own or with a naturalist on frequently scheduled trips during the summer. These are walking trails — too rough for bicycles — and no motorized vehicles are permitted. A detailed map of the entire island and a brochure of Bay Islands Park showing the trails is available at the Prudence Inn.

Several miles of paved roads follow the shore and circle the center of the island. A few bikes are available for rent at the inn, but it's best to bring your own. **Sandy Point Beach** on the east side of the island, although pebbly, is the best area for swimming.

You can see remnants of Prudence's early history as a farming and fishing community — old stone walls from sheep pens, cattle barns, and wells. A few large Victorian houses from a brief resort period are visible along the western shore. For the most part, however, the houses today are compact cottages with hammocks, rockers, and chaise longues on comfortable front porches.

About four hundred fifty year-round residents live on the island. Most are retirees, but some are younger islanders who commute to the mainland each day to work, using the recently added year-round car ferry. Some islanders, particularly those whose families have lived here for generations, view such changes as detrimental to their peaceful way of life, but others like the convenience.

In spite of the new ferry service and the recent addition of a Laundromat, life on Prudence Island seems hardly in danger of much change. Islanders continue to cherish their simple pleasures and unhurried lifestyle and plan to keep it that way. Those who take the time to seek out and find the little Whale in the Bay will be awfully glad they did.

ACCESS

BRISTOL. Directions: From I-195 follow Route 114 south to Bristol, keeping to the harbor area (Church Street). The ferry dock is on your right, and a parking lot is close by.

PRUDENCE ISLAND NAVIGATION COMPANY. Directions: Located at ferry dock, Church Street. The ferry makes several round trips each day during the summer months but fewer during the off-season. **Season:** Year-round. **Admission:** Charged. **Telephone:** (401) 245-7411.

THE ISLAND TRANSPORTATION COMPANY (car ferry). Directions: From I-195 follow Route 114 south to Melville. Turn right at the sign for Bend Boat Basin and follow the signs to the ferry. **Season:** Year-round. **Admission:** Charged. **Telephone:** (401) 683-0554.

PRUDENCE INN. Directions: The inn is close to the dock at Sandy Point. **Season:** Mid-May to mid-October. **Telephone:** (401) 683-9893.

BAY ISLANDS PARK. For information regarding group tours and the ferry shuttle *(Patriot)* to northern and southern ends of Prudence, call (401) 277-2632.

CAMPING INFORMATION. Department of Environmental Management, Division of Parks and Recreation, 83 Park Street, Providence, RI 02903; (401) 277-2632.

AUDUBON SOCIETY OF RHODE ISLAND. For information regarding special trips to Prudence Island for nature and historic walks, write to 40 Bowen Street, Providence, RI 02903, or call (401) 521-1670.

MASSACHUSETTS

This island-bound adventurer can hardly wait for his ship to come in.

Its nickname, "the Bay State," immediately suggests Massachusetts' dependence on its varied and important coastline. From the sandy shores of Cape Cod and the islands on the south, to the rocky promontory of Cape Ann on the north, fishing, boatbuilding, and shipping have been a significant part of the state's economy for centuries. Tourism, of course, has long since been added to that list.

With its long Cape Cod arm and bent finger, the coastline of Massachusetts seems to beckon the traveler to its shores. The Cape peninsula, which dominates the shoreline, extends sixty-five miles east and then north into the Atlantic Ocean. Its shape results from the constant buffeting by winds and ocean currents and the great deposits of sand, clay, and gravel left in the wake of the last Ice Age glacier.

Named by English navigator Bartholomew Gosnold in 1602 for the abundant codfish in its surrounding waters, the Cape is now one of the largest recreational attractions on the Northeast Coast. The Cape's long stretches of sandy beach backed by high dunes, protected coves and bays, and numerous freshwater lakes and ponds, are further enhanced by the presence of some of the most enchanting islands in New England, lying just off the coast.

These islands offer visitors a delectable variety of experiences. At Cuttyhunk, one of the Elizabeth Islands, a small archipelago forming the southern boundary of Buzzards Bay, anglers have been reeling in prize catches for years. Just a short hop away is a vacationer's dream, Martha's Vineyard, which accommodates everyone from the barefoot camper to the jet setter. And who hasn't heard of Nantucket, the "Little Gray Lady of the Sea," dripping with enough quaintness and nostalgia to melt the heart of the most jaded traveler.

Farther up the coast, all within view of the Boston skyline, lie the old and historic Boston Harbor Islands. Steeped in legend and lore, these primitive plots, so close to the metropolis, offer vacationers quiet places to swim, fish, camp, and explore famous national landmarks. Just before the rocky promontory of Cape Ann, with its artists' colony and fishing ports of Gloucester and Rockport, lies Plum Island. Not only does it have one of the most beautiful beaches in the state, popular with surfers, but it also encompasses an important national wildlife refuge, providing ample opportunities for bird watchers throughout the year.

If you're a well-seasoned island hopper, the islands of Massachusetts are already, no doubt, among your favorites. For the novice many wonderful secrets and surprises are just waiting to be discovered.

Elizabeth Islands (Cuttyhunk)

On the little island of **Cuttyhunk,** the westernmost in the chain of Elizabeth Islands off Cape Cod, you'll probably hear some of the biggest fish stories ever told. But unlike the legendary tales about "the one that got away," these are about the ones that didn't. Through the years world-record stripers have been reeled in from the waters around Cuttyhunk, the largest so far weighing in at almost eighty pounds.

Through the years world-record stripers have been reeled in from the waters around Cuttyhunk, the largest so far weighing in at almost eighty pounds.

Needless to say, fishing is *the* most popular sport here. In the late nineteenth century, when it was confirmed by experts that this was the best location for stripers on the East Coast, several posh striped bass fishing clubs were established in the surrounding region by wealthy sportsmen, and the Cuttyhunk Club was considered tops among the lot. Bass stands were erected all around the island, and every night in season members drew numbers to see which stand each would use the following day. Young boys were employed to "chum," first baiting the fisherman's hook, then tossing pieces of lobster tail into the surrounding waters to lure the bass. The amount of money each "chummer" earned was directly related to the size of the catch.

While there has been a marked decline in the striped bass population here during this century (fishermen blame it on the industrial pollution of Chesapeake Bay, the spawning area and nursery for most of the striped bass on the East Coast) and the old Cuttyhunk Club building is now a private residence, there are still plenty of stripers left for the sports angler. All summer the harbor is filled with a diverse assortment of crafts, from tiny sailboats to tall ships to expensive power yachts, and all are well-equipped with fishing gear.

The Elizabeth Islands, an archipelago of sixteen islands varying in size from a few acres to several thousand acres, stretch out across Buzzards Bay from Woods Hole on Cape Cod. They were discovered by the English explorer Bartholomew Gosnold in 1602, and historians continue to debate whether they were named for his queen or his sister. Most of the islands, however, still retain old Indian names such as Nashon, Nashawena, Monohansett, Uncatena, Penikese, and Pasque. Cuttyhunk is the only island with a year-round community and the only one officially open to the public. Most of the islands are privately owned — as they have been for generations — by old Boston families who glide back and forth between island and mainland on their own private yachts. One island, Penikese, which was once a leper colony, is now owned by the government and is home to the **Penikese Island**

The motorized golf cart is the transportation mode of choice among Cuttyhunk residents of all persuasions.

School. Teen-age boys, referred to the school by the Massachusetts Department of Youth Services, receive vocational training here, and since its founding in 1973, they have built a house, barn, and shop and raise and cook most of their own food.

The only public ferry (and mail boat) to serve Cuttyhunk, the ***Alert***, leaves from Leonard's Wharf in New Bedford and goes directly to Cuttyhunk. Large, square, well-built houses, their white paint and red roofs gleaming in the sun, are perched here and there atop the higher ground overlooking the harbor where the ferry docks. An enormous computerized windmill occupies the highest point of the island. Ironically the windmill proved to be too expensive to operate, so it has never been used.

Cuttyhunk has few tall trees, most of them having been chopped down and hauled away for lumber years ago. The low vegetation is a thick tangle of bayberries, wild roses, sassafras (much prized by early explorers for medicinal purposes), pitch pine, and scrub oak. It crowds the footpaths and can make hiking difficult. Fragrant wildflowers and wonderful-tasting blueberries and blackberries are profuse.

The fourteen-mile trip out takes about an hour and a half, plenty of time to get some of your questions answered by the affable Captain Ray Hopps, who has been piloting the *Alert* since 1974. The island is about three miles long and only three-fourths of a mile wide. While the summer population is about four hundred, with most of those sleeping aboard their boats in the harbor, the winter population dwindles to about a dozen families — only about twenty-five people in all.

Surprisingly, modern conveniences have graced Cuttyhunk for some time. Chalk it up to a few wealthy landowners that a small electric plant, town water and sewage systems, telephones, and television are taken for granted. Several large, lovely old homes dominate the island, and their occupants own a large share of the land.

The island has only one inn, the **Allen House**, with homey accommodations and good food. Happily, the restaurant hours coincide with ferry docking time, and every table gets a window seat on the long enclosed front veranda. Liquor is not served, but ice and setups are provided.

The **Vineyard View Bakery and Restaurant** serves a delicious chowder along with sandwiches and many breakfast and lunch specials. The island also has a well-stocked general store for picnic supplies and necessities.

As on many islands, the post office on Cuttyhunk occupies a small addition to the postmaster's house.

Just behind the Vineyard View is an interesting little gift shop, **Dot's Gifts**, run by Dot Brown. Dot's family has been summering on Cuttyhunk for several generations, and her little house and shop were made from the remains of shipwrecks that washed up on the island more than eighty years ago. She has a nice collection of hand-carved ducks, knitted articles, and jewelry, and she recently added some brass items (plaques, bottle openers, door knockers, and such) "in order to find something that would interest the men and get them to come into the shop."

The only other shop on the island is **Cuttyhunk Crafts**, run by two cousins, Kit Dennis and Kathy Olsen. Both of their families also have been summering on the island for generations. Kit and Kathy concentrate on items "that we think represent Cuttyhunk and are useful," Kit says. Clothespin baskets, shell wreaths, and T-shirts are among the items they offer. A favorite item with young customers is their "Adventure in a Bottle," a small bottle containing a form to be filled out with a message and return address. Kit's daughter Jenny got the idea when someone found a bottle she had tossed into the ocean and later wrote to her.

Only about one mile of paved road surrounds

the main section of the island, so biking is limited. One couple who had brought over bikes, however, said that it was "just enough on a hot day" because the island is very hilly. There are no cars on the island, except for the few necessary vehicles, and most islanders drive minibikes or motorized golf carts. Some carts have surreylike tops, and at least one islander has equipped hers with side curtains.

The best way to see the island is on foot, and while most of the island is private land, numerous trails are available for the careful and thoughtful hiker. The terrain includes rolling hills, grassy valleys, and meadowland, and the rocky beaches are good for beachcombing. **The Lookout** at the top of the hill up from the ferry landing affords a great view of Vineyard Sound and the colored cliffs of Gay Head on Martha's Vineyard.

Several **charter boats** are for hire, and surfcasting is permitted all along the beach. West End Pond is a good area for quahaugs, and on the bay side of the island mussels are plentiful.

The island has no golf or tennis facilities, and with the exception of some vintage movies shown each week at the town hall, there are no organized activities. The Solads, proprietors of the Allen House, state in their brochure, "Cuttyhunk is very much a do-it-yourself island. . . . Bring books, games, fishing equipment and walking shoes. . . . Everything else for a perfect vacation is here in abundance."

The Lookout Tower, Cuttyhunk's high point, affords a panoramic view of the other Elizabeth Islands, Vineyard Sound, and Martha's Vineyard's colorful Gay Head cliffs.

ACCESS

NEW BEDFORD and *ALERT*. Directions: From I-195 take exit 15, following signs to the waterfront and Pier 3 where the *Alert* is docked. Parking at the pier is free. **Season:** Year-round. **Telephone:** (617) 992-1432.

ISLAND AIR SERVICE. A small charter service (Cessna seaplanes) makes frequent trips to the island (10 minutes to Cuttyhunk from New Bedford). **Telephone:** (617) 994-1231.

ALLEN HOUSE. Directions: A short walk up the hill from the dock. Allen House provides a truck to carry your baggage. **Season:** Late May to early October (with off-season rates May/June and from mid-September to closing. **Telephone:** (617) 996-9292.

VINEYARD VIEW BAKERY AND RESTAURANT. Directions: From the ferry landing walk halfway up the hill to the sign. Turn left and follow the signs to the bakery. **Season:** Mid-May to mid-October.

DOT'S GIFTS. Directions: Walk to the top of the hill, past the Allen House. Take the first left and follow the signs. **Season:** Mid-June to mid-September.

CUTTYHUNK CRAFTS. Directions: From the ferry landing walk up the hill, taking the right turn at the fork, and follow the signs. **Season:** Mid-June to mid-September (some fall weekends).

FISHING CHARTERS. Several charter boats are available for hire. Call either the Allen House (617) 996-9292 or Cuttyhunk Wharfinger (617) 996-9215. **Season:** Mid-May to mid-October.

Martha's Vineyard

The winter is forbidden till December,
And exits March the second on the dot.
By order summer lingers through September . . .

Legend has it (with the help of Messrs. Lerner and Loewe) that the mystical place known as Camelot was a hamlet somewhere in England. But to the year-round residents and off-season visitors of Martha's Vineyard, the above lyrics might just as well describe the island they know and love.

This is one of the few northern islands that draws visitors to its shores the whole year long.

All year round, warm currents from the Gulf Stream keep the shallow waters around the Vineyard from freezing and keep the winters mild, and while you may not want to go into the ocean for a dip between November and March, this is one of the few northern islands that draws visitors to its shores the whole year long. Even in the dead of winter, in true Camelot fashion "there's a legal limit to the snow here." To quote the local chamber of commerce, "During the winter season, snowfall totals less than thirty inches. Snow cover, however, rarely lasts more than a few days because of rapid melting."

Martha's Vineyard is about twenty miles long and ten miles wide, having an area of approximately one hundred square miles. Ferries to the island sail from New Bedford, Woods Hole, Falmouth, and Hyannis. The trip is shortest from Falmouth, taking only forty minutes. If you plan to take a car you have to leave from Woods Hole (forty-five-minute ferry ride), but you must make reservations well in advance, particularly during the summer months. There are six small towns on the Vineyard — Edgartown, Oak Bluffs, Vineyard Haven (Tisbury), West

These Oak Bluffs Campground cottages are reminders of Oak Bluffs' association with the nineteenth-century evangelical revivalist movement.

Tisbury, Chilmark, and Gay Head — each with a character all its own.

The Reverend Thomas Mayhew, Jr., came in 1642, settling in what is now called Edgartown and what has been ever since the county seat. Mayhew found the Wampanoag Indians to be peaceful and helpful, and in true missionary fashion he taught them to speak English while learning their language himself. The population of the island today includes descendants of the Wampanoag, retirees, celebrities, descendants of some of the earliest white families to settle on the island, and a constant influx of young people.

Martha's Vineyard has a year-round population of about ten thousand that bulges to more than sixty-two thousand in the summer. And according to an old legend, each day, when the hundreds of day-trippers arrive, the island sinks by three inches. Tourism accounts for more than sixty percent of the island's economy. But even on the busiest day of summer all you have to do to escape the crowds is

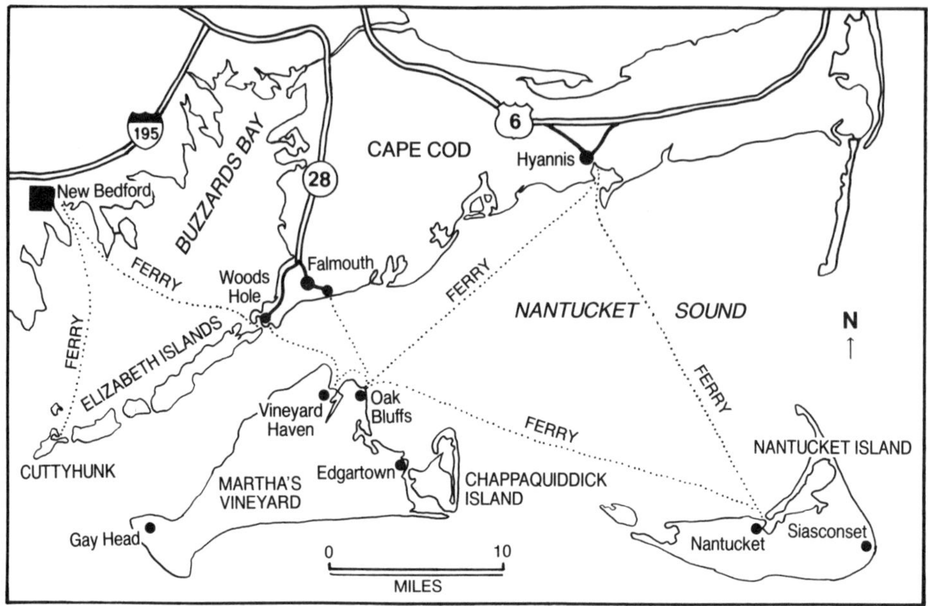

Elizabeth Islands, Martha's Vineyard, and Nantucket

take a short walk or ride to the outskirts of any of the six towns that make up the island, and chances are you will find a perfectly isolated spot. Miles of beautiful beaches, where you can find your own private sand dune, surround the island. In fact, Martha's Vineyard has more than thirty beaches, sandy ones for sunning and digging, rocky ones for climbing and exploring, beaches with gentle waves for waders or dashing waves for surfers, freshwater beaches, saltwater beaches, and beaches where you dress or undress as you prefer. Several free publications available at most stores and hotels on the island have maps and directions to the various beaches.

Tennis courts and golf courses, which are used almost year-round, are plentiful, and fishing charters start in the early spring and go through the late fall. Sailing is one of the most popular activities in the summer, with many races taking place. All types of boats are available for rent, and you can take lessons or just sit back, relax, and be taken on a cruise around the island.

Accommodations on Martha's Vineyard run from the plush **Charlotte Inn** in Edgartown to family camping grounds in both Vineyard Haven and Oak Bluffs. There is also a **youth hostel** in West Tisbury, which is popular with bicyclists. The chamber of commerce has a long list of small inns and guesthouses, some serving breakfast. One of the best reasons for visiting the island off-season is the substantial reduction in prices these places offer.

No one knows for sure how the island got its name. The Indians called it "Noe-pe," and when Italian explorer Giovanni da Verrazano sailed past it in 1524, he named it Island Louisa. Other explorers gave it different names, but English navigator Bartholomew Gosnold is credited by most historians with naming the island in 1602 for the wild grapes he found here and for his young daughter. (Another legend has it that an early explorer named the three islands in the vicinity for his three daughters, Martha, Nancy, and Naomi, hence the names, Martha's Vineyard, Nantucket, and No Mans Land. The latter, only about three miles from the southern tip of the Vineyard, is owned by the United States government and is used for naval bombing practice. It is closed to visitors.)

Edgartown, the first white settlement on Martha's Vineyard, is an elegant village, its narrow streets lined with stately white Greek Revival houses attesting to the wealth of the whaling days in the early nineteenth century. Throughout the summer some of the most expensive privately owned yachts in the country tie up in the harbor where the whaling vessels once anchored.

Interesting historic places and shops, old inns and guesthouses, and fine restaurants line the main streets of Edgartown. The best way to see the town is by strolling along North Water Street, with its row of captains' houses rich in architectural details, or South Water Street, which is dominated by a huge pagoda tree brought as a seedling from China in the early days of the last century by one of the captains. While many of these homes are still lived in, many are open to the public all summer. The oldest house on the island is the **Vincent House**, built in 1672 and occupied by descendants of the same family until 1977. The **Old Whaling Church**, built in 1843 and now the Performing Arts Center, is well worth a visit. Shoppers will delight in an eclectic array of shops along the little roads leading down to the harbor or tucked into small side streets. Knitters will love a shop called **Outrageous**, just behind the courthouse on Main Street. The shop has an unusual collection of imported designer yarns and makes sweaters to order. A particularly popular ice cream shop, **Mad Martha's Ice Cream Factory** (with a second location in Oak Bluffs), just off Main Street

Throughout the summer some of the most expensive privately owned yachts in the country tie up in the harbor where the whaling vessels once anchored.

on North Water, has more than two dozen flavors from which to choose and offers the Banana Ferry for the hearty appetite. If you're hungry for a good cup of real New England clam chowder, try **The Wharf**, where you can sit outside (in good weather) or at the indoor bar.

The Oak Bluffs **Methodist Campgrounds and Tabernacle** document an important period in Martha's Vineyard history. Until the mid-1880s, the island's economy depended almost entirely on whaling. But with the discovery of petroleum, making whale oil obsolete, and with the capture of most of the Edgartown whaling fleet by the Confederate navy during the Civil War, Martha's Vineyard faced a bleak future. Just about this time, however, a whole new industry began taking shape on the outskirts of Edgartown in an area that is now the separate town of Oak Bluffs. An evangelical revivalist movement was sweeping the country, and a group of Methodists had begun to hold their camp meetings in an oak grove high on the bluffs at the northern end of Edgartown. It turned out to be the beginning of the first summer resort on the Vineyard.

The summer meetings began in 1835. Methodist ministers conducted services in the open air, and followers pitched their tents in the area around where services were held. Camp meetings of this sort were going on all over New England, but the beauty of Oak Bluffs kept ministers and followers coming back each year.

Because cottages were limited in size, owners began to decorate them with Victorian ornamentations — scalloped shingles Lilliputian balconies and turrets — and to paint them in riotous colors.

By 1859 the Martha's Vineyard Camp Meeting had become the largest in the world, with more than twelve thousand visitors in attendance. People began to replace their tents with tiny cottages small enough to fit on a single tent lot. Because cottages were limited in size, owners began to decorate them with Victorian ornamentations — scalloped shingles and Lilliputian balconies and turrets — and to paint them in riotous colors. People then began to stay on throughout the summer after revival meetings had ended, and soon hotels, dance halls, and an enormous boardwalk were built.

A large, all-steel tabernacle was built in 1879 to replace the enormous circuslike tent that had been used for revival meetings. It still stands today but is more commonly used for community events, high-school graduation ceremonies, concerts, and summer-long entertainment culminating with Illumination Night.

Illumination Night was first celebrated in 1869 and occurs annually on a night in mid-August.

For the occasion, Oriental lanterns are hung from every conceivable place — ceilings, porches, windows, trees, even picket fences. At the conclusion of a rousing community sing held in the tabernacle, an elderly citizen who has been chosen ahead of time lights the first lantern, and with the shout from the leader, "Let the lanterns be lit," hundreds of lights blaze into life simultaneously throughout the tabernacle and across the campgrounds. It is a spectacular sight!

The Secret Garden, a fascinating shop on Circuit Avenue and close to the entrance to the campgrounds, is filled with all sorts of interesting things. The shop has an unusual collection of dolls and children's books, hand-painted window blinds from the Orient, wicker furniture, and colorful gift wrappings and greeting cards. Everything is displayed in a colorful cottage that looks like it just escaped from the campgrounds.

The **Flying Horse Carousel** is another special Oak Bluffs attraction. It's the oldest operating carousel in the country and one of only two that still feature the brass ring game (if you catch the brass ring you get a free ride). Also, it's under cover, which makes for a nice rainy-day activity.

For strollers, browsers, and shoppers, the streets of Edgartown provide one delightful discovery after another.

In Chilmark, on the opposite end of the island, farming is still evident, and the miles of unusual stone walls (the stones are arranged to let the wind rush through, giving them a fragile, almost lacy appearance), marking farm boundaries as well as serving to restrain wandering animals, are a delight to see. Chilmark, along with Tisbury and Gay Head, are referred to as "up island," while Vineyard Haven, Oak Bluffs, and Edgartown are "down island." Up island, which few tourists take the time to see, is where you'll find the **Allen Farm Sheep & Wool Company**. It is one of the island's oldest working farms, where sheep have been raised for more than two hundred years. The Allens (including Clarissa Allen, who lives in her family's two-hundred-year-old farmhouse) not only raise sheep but also take the fleece to a finished product, hand-dying the yarns and then weaving them into beautiful, soft blankets and throws. They also make, to order, hand-knitted sweaters, vests, shawls, and scarves. The shop is located in the old farmhouse on the South Road in Chilmark and is open year-round. (The farm itself is not open for touring.)

Menemsha, a small village in Chilmark on Vineyard Sound, is the last of the real fishing villages on the island. It has been the subject of countless paintings and photographs by the artists and photographers attracted to this area each summer. This has been the scene of many shipwrecks, and the Coast Guard station is located here. Years before the station was established, Menemsha fishermen themselves often volunteered for heroic lifesaving missions when ships were in trouble off these shores. Along the dock you can buy freshly caught fish, and there's good swimming and beachcombing at the public beach close by. So scenic is this little harbor that it is a favorite painting spot for artists and also has been used as the backdrop for several movies, including *Jaws* and *Jaws II*.

So scenic is this little harbor that it is a favorite painting spot for artists and also has been used as the backdrop for several movies, including Jaws *and* Jaws II.

The ferries from Falmouth and Woods Hole dock in Vineyard Haven, which is the port area and business district of Tisbury. Here you will have the opportunity to visit the **Seamen's Bethel**, a chapel and museum, once a place for weary sailors and now one of the oldest buildings in town. Then stop by the town hall, where, on the second floor, you'll find the **Katherine Cornell Memorial Theater**. Mrs. Cornell, a widely known actress and producer during the 1930s and 1940s, and her husband had a home in Tisbury and spent several months each year on the island. She donated money to have the building renovated and, hiring her own architect, had the second floor made into a theater where local artists put on polished theatrical productions throughout the year.

In Menemsha, Martha's Vineyard's last true fishing village, you're old enough to cast a line when you're old enough to bait a hook.

A most unusual museum to visit is **Windfarm** on Edgartown–Vineyard Haven Road. Here you will see ancient as well as modern windmills, working methods of harnessing the sun and wind for everyday use, a fishpond with underwater viewing windows, and many hands-on exhibits.

Along with the wild grapes still found on the island (and several varieties of wild berries), thirty acres of cultivated grapes are produced at the **Chicama Vineyards** on the Old County Road outside Vineyard Haven. Visitors are welcome, and daily tours of the Chicama Winery are available. While you're out this way be sure to stop by the **Scottish Bakehouse**, one of the most charming bakeries you're apt to run across. It's run by Isabella White, who came to the Vineyard more than twenty years ago with a suitcase full of traditional Scottish recipes. Along with a wonderful selection of breads, cakes, and cookies (and a shortbread that melts in your mouth), Isabella offers her recipes in a beautifully illustrated volume, *The Scottish Bakehouse Cook Book.*

No trip to Martha's Vineyard would be complete without a visit to the magnificent **Gay Head Cliffs** located west of Chilmark in Gay Head. Years ago, before there was even a road out to this part of the island, visitors would walk, sometimes taking two days to make the journey. Now you can drive or bike on a good road to see these spectacular cliffs, which rise up to a height of more than one hundred fifty feet, exposing a brilliant array of colors from dark browns to pink and bright orange to pure white. No matter how many times you see them, they are always different. Unfortunately that is due to the erosion taking place at a rate of four to six feet a year. The lighthouse that sits atop the cliffs, the second largest on the East Coast, has had to be moved twice because of the erosion.

No trip to Martha's Vineyard would be complete without a visit to the magnificent Gay Head Cliffs.

Gay Head is one of the two Indian townships in Massachusetts (the other is Mashpee on Cape Cod). Many year-round and summer residents of Gay Head are descendants of the Wampanoag Indians, who lived on the island long before the white settlers. On the short path to the cliffs you will find a row of small Indian-owned shops selling souvenirs, gifts and food. Also here is the popular **Aquinnah Restaurant,** with a deck overlooking the cliffs.

There is almost no end to the sights to see, places to go, and things to do on the Vineyard, and the best way to take advantage of them is to arm

Before a road was built to make the ever-changing cliffs of Gay Head easily accessible, sightseers sometimes hiked for two days to view the spectacular attraction.

yourself with a free map and a bike or a moped and take off on your own. Bicycles, mopeds, and automobiles can be rented in Vineyard Haven, Oak Bluffs, and Edgartown and at the airport in Tisbury. Reasonably priced shuttle buses run between the towns as well, but the interval between buses is sometimes quite long. If you're short on time, numerous bus tours and taxis are available to take you around the island. Taxis are about as expensive as they are in any major city.

To those in the know, off-season has become the best time to visit the island. The crowds are gone, and you can ride for miles on bike paths and bridle trails without constantly having to steer out of someone's way. The foliage, if it's not glorious with fall colors or laced with spring blossoms, has disappeared altogether, leaving expansive, breathtaking panoramas of the sea not visible when summer greenery is at its height.

Special events occur throughout the off-season months, such as the annual **Striped Bass and Bluefish Derby** from mid-September to mid-October. More than two thousand contestants of all ages and from all over the country compete for prizes. **Tivoli Day,** held in Oak Bluffs in mid-September, features a street fair, bike races, and a mini fishing derby and is eagerly anticipated by both local and visiting children. And during the Christmas season in Edgartown the narrow streets and lanes glitter with Christmas lights and decorations. Carolers burst into song at the slightest invitation, and the local pubs are filled every evening with their voices.

In spring, when the fields are covered with bright yellow Scotch broom, bird watchers come from far and wide to catch a glimpse of unusual and rare species of migratory birds that touch down on the island for a rest. Wild geese, turkeys, and peacocks roam the wildlife sanctuaries in **Felix Neck** in Edgartown and **Cape Pogue Wildlife Reservation** on Chappaquiddick, while herons and snowy egrets line the banks of Herring Creek. Observation and photography blinds are strategically placed in the bird sanctuaries.

Chappaquiddick, so named by the Wampanoag Indians and meaning "separated island," is part of the town of Edgartown. A one-hundred-twenty-yard channel separates the two, and the crossing takes less than five minutes. The island is an ideal place to take a bike, as the best beaches are three miles across the island from where the ferry lands. (Caution: thick patches of particularly virulent forms of poison ivy and poison sumac grow everywhere.) **East Beach,** an ocean beach, and **Wasque Point,** where you can enjoy the waters of **Pocha Pond** and **Katama Bay** as well as the ocean, are part of **Cape Pogue Wildlife Refuge and Wasque Reservation.** In the summer a guard is on duty at both beaches, and a nominal fee for swimming and parking is collected.

A few residents live here year-round, and although there are many summer people as well, this tiny island always seems quiet and secluded. There are no public facilities or accommodations on Chappaquiddick.

To those in the know, off-season has become the best time to visit the island.

The mild winter weather and the beauty and variety of the landscape make Martha's Vineyard truly an island for all seasons. Visitors return year after year, some searching for the low-key, unhurried lifestyle found on a quiet lane in Chilmark, and others seeking out the bustling villages of Edgartown and Oak Bluffs. Whatever your island pleasure, you're sure to find it on this, the largest island in New England.

ACCESS

WOODS HOLE (STEAMSHIP AUTHORITY). Directions: Take I-195 north to Route 28, following "Cape and Islands" signs. Cross the Bourne Bridge to Cape Cod. Continue south on Route 28 to Falmouth. The parking lot for passengers is on your right. This parking lot is 4 miles from Woods Hole, but a free shuttle bus runs continually to the ferry landing. There is a fee to park your car here. If you are taking your car aboard the ferry, continue south on Route 28 to Woods Hole Road. Follow Woods Hole road to the ferry dock, on your left. **Season:** Year-round. **Admission:** Charged. **Telephone:** (617) 540-2022.

Note: From May through September several other ferry services go to Martha's Vineyard. Call the following for schedules:

Cape & Islands Express Lines, Inc. (New Bedford) (617) 997-1688
Hy-Line, Inc. (Hyannis) (617) 775-7185
Island Queen (Falmouth) (617) 548-4800
Schamonchi (New Bedford) (617) 997-1688

AIRLINE SERVICE. Several airlines have service to Martha's Vineyard. Call the following for schedules:

Business Express (White Plains, NY) (800) 243-9830
Gull Air (Boston and Hyannis) (617) 771-1247
Provincetown-Boston Airlines, Inc. (Boston, New York City, Cape Cod) (617) 487-0240

OUTRAGEOUS. Directions: Located in Post Office Square, Edgartown, right behind the courthouse off Main Street. **Season:** Year-round. **Telephone:** (617) 627-5053.

MAD MARTHA'S ICE CREAM FACTORY. Directions: In Oak Bluffs walk up Oak Bluffs Avenue from the ferry to Circuit Avenue. Mad Martha's is on the left-hand side of Circuit Avenue. In Edgartown, it is located just off Main Street, on the right side of North Water Street. **Season:** Mid-June through Labor Day. **Telephone:** (617) 693-0366.

METHODIST CAMPGROUNDS AND TABERNACLE. Directions: From the ferry landing in Oak Bluffs walk up Oak Bluffs Avenue to Circuit Avenue. About halfway up on the right, between some small shops, is the arcade leading into the campgrounds. **Season:** Year-round. **Admission:** Free. **Telephone:** (617) 693-0068.

THE SECRET GARDEN. Directions: From the ferry landing in Oak Bluffs walk up Oak Bluffs Avenue to Circuit Avenue, and just before the entrance to the Methodist Campgrounds you will see a colorful gingerbread cottage on your right. **Season:** Early spring through Christmas. **Admission:** Free. **Telephone:** (617) 693-4759.

FLYING HORSE CAROUSEL. Directions: From the ferry landing in Oak Bluffs walk up Oak Bluffs Avenue to the main square. The carousel is directly across the street. **Season:** Year-round. **Admission:** Charged.

ALLEN FARM SHEEP & WOOL COMPANY. Directions: Take State Road from Vineyard Haven (from Edgartown take the Edgartown–West Tisbury Road) about 10 miles to South Road. Follow South Road toward Chilmark. The farm is on the right side on South Road. **Season:** Year-round. **Admission:** Free. **Telephone:** (617) 645-9064.

KATHERINE CORNELL MEMORIAL THEATER. Di-

Edgartown, as seen from Chappaquiddick, is a picture postcard island village.

rections: From the ferry landing in Vineyard Haven walk up Union Street, taking a left onto Main Street. Spring Street, where the town hall (theater is on the second floor) is located, is the second right. **Season:** Year-round. **Admission:** Charged (if there is a show). **Telephone (town hall):** (617) 693-4200.

WINDFARM. Directions: Take State Road from Vineyard Haven and turn left onto Edgartown–Vineyard Haven Road. Windfarm is on your left. **Season:** Mid-June through early September. **Admission:** Charged. **Telephone:** (617) 693-3658.

CHICAMA VINEYARDS. Directions: Take State Road from Vineyard Haven for about two and a half miles. A sign to the vineyards is on the left. Turn onto Stoney Hill Road and drive to the end. **Season:** Early spring through fall and by appointment the rest of the year. **Admission:** Free. **Telephone:** (617) 693-0309.

SCOTTISH BAKEHOUSE. Directions: Take State Road out of Vineyard Haven for about 2 miles. The bakery is on your right. **Season:** Year-round. **Admission:** Free. **Telephone:** (617) 693-1873.

MARTHA'S VINEYARD CHAMBER OF COMMERCE. Beach Road, Vineyard Haven, MA 02568; (617) 693-0085.

CHAPPAQUIDDICK ISLAND. Directions: From Main Street in Edgartown go directly to the harbor area, where you will see signs to Town Wharf. The ferry *On Time* makes continual crossings from early morning to late night. **Season:** Year-round. **Admission:** Charged. **Telephone:** (617) 627-9794 or 627-5391.

CAPE POGUE WILDLIFE REFUGE. Directions: From the ferry dock continue straight ahead on the paved road (about 2½ miles). As the paved road veers to the right, continue straight ahead on the dirt road, crossing Dyke

Bridge. A path leads down to the beach. **Season:** Year-round. **Admission:** Charged. **Telephone (Trustees of Reservations):** (617) 627-8644.

Nantucket

Nantucketers, who cherish their insularity and closely guard their identity as islanders, often refer to the mainland (and not always in jest) as America.

Nantucket, its very name a corruption of the Indian word Nanticut, meaning "faraway land," lies thirty miles out to sea and is one of the islands farthest off the coast of New England to maintain a thriving year-round population. Its distance from the mainland gives it a special charm — a sense of isolation — which has attracted visitors for centuries. And Nantucketers, who cherish their insularity and closely guard their identity as islanders, often refer to the mainland (and not always in jest) as America.

A walk along the island's cobbled Main Street is a revelation in the importance and prosperity of the whaling industry that once thrived here. As early as 1740 and continuing for almost a century Nantucket was the leading whaling port in the world. Wealthy fleet owners and captains made fortunes from sperm oil and poured much of their money into building stately homes that line most of the streets throughout the village. Among the homes you see along Main Street are "the three bricks," identical houses built by Joseph Starbuck, a prosperous shipowner, for his three sons, George, Matthew, and William. Built in the 1830s, they are named **West Brick, Middle Brick,** and **East Brick,** and most architectural historians refer to them as the most perfect examples of colonial Georgian architecture found in the country. The two impressive pillared mansions just across the street were built by partners in a sperm-oil factory who married two of Starbuck's daughters.

While one of these two houses and several others in the village are today maintained by the **Nantucket Historical Association** and are open to the public, most of the homes along Main Street, with their gleaming silver knockers and nameplates, are privately owned.

Some of the interesting things you'll see on a tour of the homes operated by the association are fine examples of Regency, Empire, and Victorian furnishings and beautifully maintained gardens authentic to 1850s landscaping. Be sure to look for the mortgage button on the bottom of the bannister at the **Hadwen House** (96 Main Street). When early

Not even modern-day utility lines can detract from the splendor of these pillared mansions on Nantucket's cobblestoned Main Street.

houses were built on Nantucket the owner would plant an ivory button on the bottom post of the staircase as soon as he had finished paying for his house. In the museum shop next to the Whaling Museum you can find reproductions of these mortgage buttons for your own home.

You'll also find many of the houses along the streets of Nantucket ornamented with brass pineapples on their doors and fence posts. This symbol of welcome, which dates back to the eighteenth century, was started by Nantucket whalers. The pineapple was then considered a rare delicacy that whalers brought back from the Pacific islands. On their return, they would display a pineapple on their fence post to signify their return as well as an invitation to friends and neighbors to come and "share the fruit."

Since the turn of the century, wealthy summer residents have held sway here. Unlike Newport, with its marble and glitter, or Martha's Vineyard, with its elaborate gingerbread, Nantucket has maintained a simple elegance. It was settled mainly by Quakers, whose beliefs in plain and uncomplicated living dominated the island for nearly two hundred years. Today Nantucket has a Historic District Commission that keeps a tight rein on all construction and alteration of buildings on the island. While lower Main Street and many of its little alleys and lanes are filled with shops, restaurants, and guesthouses, an owner must get a permit if he or she wants to change so much as the shape of a sign over a door.

The simplicity of the Quakers and the grandeur of the wealthy sea merchants represent but one of the vivid contrasts that characterize this island. Only a few miles outside the flourishing seaport of Nantucket Town lie the low-growing moors that stretch — vivid green in summer, flaming red in fall — as far as the eye can see. Only here and there are they dotted with antique shingled cottages, weathered to the soft silvery gray that gives the island its nickname, "Little Gray Lady of the Sea."

Once past the moors (now part of the island's conservation area, which includes more than forty percent of the island), you come to another thriving community, **Siasconset**, or 'Sconset as the islanders call it. In the seventeenth century, 'Sconset was a cluster of little fishing shacks tossed together by fishermen as minimal protection against the elements. The fishermen had discovered the rich fishing grounds just a short distance offshore and came out each summer to catch great hauls of cod or flounder.

Eventually wives and children began to join the fishermen, bringing curtains, bedspreads, and other domestic trappings, and thus the little shacks began to take on a new look. Small additions, called "warts," were added, and before long a small but regular summer colony developed around the one and only town pump. The remoteness and charm of the spot attracted vacationers as well as fishermen, particularly artists and theater people, and while those summer people are gone now the main street is still called Broadway.

The simplicity of the Quakers and the grandeur of the wealthy sea merchants represent but one of the vivid contrasts that characterize this island.

Many of the original fishing shacks still exist, but you would hardly recognize them. Ells and wings, porches and courtyards, formal shrubs and riotous gardens have been added, to say nothing of changes to the interiors. Steep, carpeted staircases and slanted floors, their wide boards polished to a high gleam and strewn with colorful hand-hooked rugs, are a couple of clues to the houses' original structure. They're all gussied up now with English antiques, reproduced wallpaper, and crystal chandeliers, but the "shacks" are still fascinating to see. Every summer the local garden club sponsors a house tour, and several "shacks" are open for viewing. Before you start to pack your bags to move out here, however, you might like to know that these little shacks now constitute some of the most valuable pieces of real estate on the island. They rarely come on the market, and when they do the price is usually in the high six-figure bracket.

It is hard to believe that these charming and well-appointed residences are direct descendants of the crude shacks built by seventeenth-century fishermen.

Nantucket is truly an island with something for everyone. Throughout the summer months and well into the off-season, all fifty-one square miles of the island act as a sparkling magnet, drawing a constant flow of visitors. The year-round population of approximately five thousand increases tenfold from June through September.

The beaches, of course, hold the biggest attraction in summer. The island has miles and miles of them — crowded or quiet — for surfers or waders. Just a short walk from town is **Children's Beach**, a favorite with young families, and **Jetties Beach,** where lockers, changing rooms, lifeguards, and swimming instructions are available.

Boat rentals, sailing, and fishing — whether surfcasting or charters — are all close at hand. Two public nine-hole golf courses and both public and private tennis courts are available. Horseback riding on moorland trails and along the beaches is fun year-round.

Bikes and mopeds (many rentals) are the most popular ways of getting around the island. Nantucket stretches about six miles in either direction east or west from Nantucket Town, and there are good bicycle paths to follow. Another bike path leads two and a half miles out to Surfside on the south shore where the **Star of the Sea Youth Hostel** is located. The hostel has a bed capacity of seventy-two and welcomes groups.

During the summer months rental cars and taxis are fairly numerous, and many tour buses meet each incoming ferry. If you're traveling alone or in a

History buffs will find a treasure around every corner — with or without a tour.

small group, you might want to take a tour in one of the smaller **VW buses** parked just outside Robinson's Five & Ten, a short walk from the ferry dock. They are owned and operated by local residents, usually natives, who know the island well.

One of the first streets on which your tour bus will travel is **Center Street** just off Main Street. Center Street is lined with small shops and restaurants, and during the whaling days it was called **Petticoat Row** because when the men went off to sea, the women were left behind to tend the many shops and businesses that thrived there. Often as not the men never returned, and the women continued to run their businesses quite successfully.

Nantucket has produced a number of outstanding women, most notably Lucretia Mott, a Quaker minister, abolitionist, and pioneer in the women's rights movement; Abiah Franklin, who married a widower with seven children and then proceeded to have ten more of her own, one of whom was Benjamin; and Maria Mitchell, America's first woman astronomer, who in 1847 discovered a new comet and who was the first woman elected to the American Academy of Arts and Sciences. The latter's home and observatory are now part of the **Maria Mitchell Association,** which also includes a science library, a museum of natural science, and an aquarium. Throughout the summer the association conducts an extensive program of astronomy lectures along with observations at the Loines Observatory; birding, wildflower, and nature walks; and nature classes. A special lecture series on astronomy and classes in nature study are conducted for children.

Nantucket is the natural home for a whaling museum.

History buffs will find a treasure around every corner — with or without a tour — as there are museums, open houses, monuments, and exhibits all over the island. The **Whaling Museum** exhibits an outstanding collection of relics dramatically chronicling the saga of whaling expeditions. The skeleton of a forty-three-foot finback whale that washed ashore on Nantucket in 1967 extends almost the full length of the Whale Room. Accompanying photos detail the salvaging operations.

The oldest operating **windmill** in the country, built in 1746 of timbers from wrecked vessels, still grinds corn, and the cornmeal is made into delicious breads and muffins that are served in local restaurants. After watching the miller grind the corn between massive millstones, you can buy the meal itself on the premises.

The shops along Main Street, the wharfs, and the small alleys of downtown Nantucket provide an interesting look at the talent and creativity of island artisans. One of the more popular items is a "genuine" Nantucket lightship basket, a craft begun in the 1800s by crew members of the lightships anchored off Nantucket to warn the incoming ships of the dangerous shoals. (A lightship is a kind of floating lighthouse.) To wile away the many long hours, sailors wove sturdy round and oval-shaped lidded baskets to bring home to their families. The baskets were woven from Javanese or Malaysian cane, and each basket's lid was usually decorated with a small piece of scrimshaw.

Gerald Brown carries on an island tradition with the weaving of Nantucket lightship baskets.

This craft has been handed down from generation to generation, and today the baskets are often made into handbags. Gerald Brown has a workshop and studio **(Nantucket Lightship Baskets)** on Straight Wharf and has been weaving baskets for about fifteen years. He learned the art from his father. "My father added his own special touch to our baskets," he says as he proudly shows the bottom of the handle. "He added finger grips here." While Gerry spends his winters weaving baskets, his father provides the beautiful scrimshaw carvings that decorate the lids. Gerry is usually at his workshop during the summer and enjoys sharing his craft with interested observers.

Another interesting craft shop and retail store is **Nantucket Looms,** farther up Main Street. Here you can watch Annie Bessinger, one of the weavers, making lovely, soft blankets and shawls. Annie has been weaving "well — on and off for about eighteen years." Yarn seems to fall magically into the proper grooves beneath her graceful fingers.

Just up the street from Nantucket Looms is **The Sweet Shop** ("Open seven days a week from 11 A.M. till after the movie"), a favorite spot, particularly with young children. Along with the sandwiches and salads available here, you can make your own sundaes and watch them make their own ice cream.

One end of **Straight Wharf** is lined with artists' studios, and it's amazing to see the many ways in which these talented people interpret their beloved island. Young Englishman Kerry Hallam sees Nantucket in bold strokes of primary colors — an Impressionist seascape. In direct contrast, native islander Marshal DuBock uses soft pastels to portray a quiet, empty Main Street with light, feathery elms and worn cobblestones.

One end of Straight Wharf is lined with artists' studios, and it's amazing to see the many ways in which these talented people interpret their beloved island.

Nantucket is another of the northern islands

Old-fashioned cobblestone streets have long been part of Nantucket's unique charm.

that enjoys a fairly good schedule of events throughout the off-season. In September (when hotel rates go down) the waters off the shallow coast are still warm enough for swimming. Columbus Day weekend in October is full of activities: An annual **ten-mile road race** from 'Sconset and the **Artist Association's Art Auction** are both popular events. Many restaurants offer a traditional Thanksgiving banquet, and the holiday spirit continues right through to Christmas, with Main Street aglow with lights and decorations.

Since its inception in 1977, the **Christmas Stroll** has become a tradition on the island. Late in the afternoon on the second Saturday of December, the pealing of the carillon bells at the First Congregational Church signals the beginning of the stroll. A local official flips a switch lighting up the Christmas trees (which have been decorated by schoolchildren and Girl and Boy Scout groups) that line Main Street. Many shops prepare special refreshments for the occasion, musical groups perform in the street (which has been blocked off to traffic), and the Pacific Club at the foot of Main Street, a historic building that was once a meeting place for whalers and is now home to the Nantucket Chamber of Commerce, features a huge "talking tree" just outside its door. Children, as well as some adults, enjoy holding conversations with the tree (thanks to windows, wires, and microphones, which allow those on the inside to see and communicate undetected). Santa Claus also shows up to join the stroll and talk to the children.

Excellent accommodations in several price ranges are available on the island throughout the year, but reservations for the summer months fill up quickly. The majority of inns and guesthouses are clustered around Nantucket Harbor, where everything is within walking distance. Nightlife includes dining and dancing, piano and jazz bars, concerts, theater, movies, dance performances, and more.

One very special activity not to be overlooked occurs each August. The annual **sandcastle contest** has grown so popular that you have to preregister to enter. If you're interested strictly in viewing, you need only show up to be amazed.

ACCESS

WOODS HOLE (STEAMSHIP AUTHORITY). Directions: Take I-195 to Route 28, following "Cape and Islands" signs. Cross the Bourne Bridge to Cape Cod, continuing south on Route 28 to Falmouth. The parking lot for passengers is on your right. This parking lot is 4 miles from Woods Hole, but a free shuttle bus runs continually to the ferry landing. There is a parking fee. If you are taking your car aboard the ferry (with advance reservations only), continue south on Route 28 to Woods Hole Road. Follow Woods Hole Road to the ferry dock, on your left. **Season:** Year-round. **Admission:** Charged. **Telephone:** (617) 540-2022.

HYANNIS (HY-LINE). Directions: From I-195 follow "Cape and Islands" signs and cross the Sagamore Bridge in Bourne. Follow Route 6 to exit 6, Hyannis. Take Route 132 to the Airport Rotary. Take the second right off the rotary, which is Barnstable Road (it becomes Ocean Street). Follow Ocean Street directly to the Hy-Line Wharf and parking lot (fee). **Season:** Late April through October. **Admission:** Charged. **Telephone:** (617) 775-7185.

AIRLINE SERVICE. Several airlines have service to Nantucket Island. Call the following for schedules:

- **Brockway Air** (Burlington, VT, and upstate NY) (800) 451-3432 or (800) 338-9100
- **Business Express** (Bridgeport, CT) (800) 243-9830 or (800) 972-9830
- **Gull Air** (Hyannis) (800) 222-4855
- **Provincetown-Boston Airlines, Inc.** (Hyannis) (800) 722-3597
- **Will's Air** (Hyannis) (800) 352-7559

NANTUCKET HISTORICAL ASSOCIATION. For information on museums, historic houses, and exhibits, write to Box 1016-2 Union Street, Nantucket, MA 02554. **Season:** Year-round. **Admission:** Charged. **Telephone:** (617) 228-1894.

MARIA MITCHELL SCIENCE CENTER, HOUSE, AND OBSERVATORY. Directions: Walk directly up Main Street from the wharf area to Vestal Street. The center is on the corner of Vestal and Milk streets. **Season:** Year-round. **Admission:** Charged. **Telephone:** (617) 228-9198.

WHALING MUSEUM. Directions: From the ferry landing at Straight Wharf, turn right onto Easy Street. Turn left onto Broad Street (third intersection), and the museum is a short distance along on your right. **Season:** Late April through October and off-season as posted. **Admission:** Charged. **Telephone:** (617) 228-1894.

NANTUCKET LIGHTSHIP BASKETS. Directions: Located on the left side (from ferry) of Straight Wharf. **Season:** May through September. **Telephone:** (617) 228-4894 or 334-6331.

NANTUCKET LOOMS. Directions: Walk up Main Street from the wharf area. The shop is on the left side of the street. **Season:** Year-round. **Telephone:** (617) 228-1908.

THE SWEET SHOP. Directions: Main Street, on the left side, just past Nantucket Looms. **Season:** June to mid-September. **Telephone:** (617) 228-1282.

NANTUCKET CHAMBER OF COMMERCE. Lower Main Street, Nantucket, MA 02554; (617) 228-1700.

Boston Harbor Islands

For those of you who have not quite made up your minds whether island hopping is for you, this is the perfect place to start.

The Boston Harbor Islands are for beginners. For those of you who have not quite made up your minds whether island hopping is for you, this is the perfect place to start. Within minutes of leaving the noisy, crowded streets of downtown Boston, you can hop aboard a ferry at Long Wharf and be sailing out of the inner harbor toward the seclusion of one of more than a dozen small, quiet island retreats.

As the Boston skyline recedes and the cacophony of city noises gives way to the mournful cry of herring gulls and the gentle slap of waves against the boat, you'll feel yourself almost instantly metamorphosed from city slicker to island adventurer. But if playing Robinson Crusoe for an hour or so on one of the islands leaves you longing to get back to the asphalt jungle (you'll really never be out of sight of the Boston skyline anyway), you can hop another ferry and be back in town almost before you can say "Swiss Family Robinson."

You might want to ride out to the islands and back just to hear some of the stories told by captains of the various cruise boats — tales of pirates and buried treasure, of lonely ghosts and unsolved murders, of tragic shipwrecks and heroic rescues, and, of course, of American history.

For the island-hopping city slicker, the reassuring sight of Boston's skyline is always visible from the Boston Harbor Islands.

Boston Harbor encompasses about fifty square miles, from Dorchester Bay to Hingham Bay, and within that area lie approximately thirty islands. The islands vary in size from a tiny outcrop of bedrock called Little Calf Island to the thickly forested 213-acre Long Island. Many bear such picturesque names as Hangman, Bumpkin, The Graves, or Spectacle. Some occupy prominent places in the history of early settlements in Massachusetts, a few even predating the founding of Boston by several years.

Thompson Island, for instance, was explored by Myles Standish and a group of Plymouth Bay colonists in 1621 and settled as early as 1626 by David Thompson. Thompson brought his family to the island, established a trading post to do business exchanging beaver furs for European goods with

Castle Island's Fort Independence is one of America's oldest fortifications.

the Neponset Indians, and, in 1626, built the first permanent building in Boston Harbor.

On **Little Brewster**, a mere slip of an island on the outer edge of the harbor, stands the famous 105-foot Boston Light. Established in 1716, it is the oldest light station in North America and one of the few still operated (by the U.S. Coast Guard). The first lighthouse, built here in 1716 and illuminated by tallow candles and wicks dipped in fish oil, was blown up by the British in 1776 as they evacuated Boston. Because of the island's strategic importance, a new lighthouse was built in 1783 and an addition was constructed in 1859. It is this lighthouse that you see today. Although **Boston Light** has been declared a National Historic Landmark, it is not currently open to the public full time.

Throughout the early history of the country and continuing into this century, the Boston Harbor Islands have played an important part in the country's national defense. One of the oldest military fortifications in the United States, **Fort Independence,** stands on Castle Island. **Fort Warren,** on George's Island, served as an important Confederate prison camp during the Civil War, housing such famous prisoners as Alexander Stephens, the vice president of the Confederacy. **Fort Strong,** whose crumbling bunkers and batteries are remnants of the Civil War, is still visible on Long Island. It remained active throughout the two world wars and served as a missile base during the 1950s.

During the late eighteenth and early nineteenth centuries, many of the islands were privately owned. Some enjoyed a brief heyday as fashionable resorts. Excursion boats from the city ferried revelers to the islands to enjoy "banned in Boston" attractions such as gambling and boxing matches. Police raids soon put a damper on these activities, however, and as business declined, buildings fell into disrepair and eventually were abandoned.

Throughout most of the nineteenth century and well into the twentieth, the islands were used as a dumping ground for society's outcasts. Prisons and asylums were erected on some, hospitals for contagious diseases on one, a home for indigent boys on another, and poorhouses (one designated for "female paupers") on yet others. One island, **Spectacle** (originally named for having the shape of a pair of eyeglasses), became a true dumping ground — a city dump — after first serving as the site of a horse slaughterhouse.

Today a massive plan has been undertaken by state and city agencies to rescue and restore the islands, not only for conservation but also for recreational and educational purposes. Most of the islands are now publicly owned and have been incorporated into **Boston Harbor Islands (BHI) State Park.** Some are managed by the Department of Environmental Management (DEM) and others by the Metropolitan District Commission (MDC). Although Thompson Island is part of the park system, it is privately owned and operated by the Thompson Island Education Center.

Aside from opportunities to explore numerous forts and archaeological remains, the islands offer recreational facilities for swimming, picnicking,

Boston Harbor Islands At-a-Glance	Bumpkin	Castle	Gallops	George's	Grape	Long	Lovell's	Peddocks	Thompson
Managed by MDC		X		X		X	X	X	
Managed by DEM	X		X		X				
Camping	X				X		X	X	
Swimming	X		X		X	X	X	X	X
Lifeguard							X		X
Picnicking	X	X	X	X	X	X	X	X	X
Trails/Paths	X	X	X	X	X	X	X	X	X
Boat piers	X	X	X	X	X		X	X	X
Fishing piers	X	X	X	X	X		X	X	X
Island manager on duty	X		X		X		X	X	
Information center				X				X	X
Guided walks	X	X	X	X	X		X	X	X
Refreshment stand		X		X				X	
Rest room facilities (some primitive)	X	X	X	X	X		X	X	X
Accessible by ferry from Boston				X				X	X
Accessible by water taxi from George's	X		X		X		X	X	

fishing, birding, hiking, guided nature walks, camping, and boating. Seven are serviced by ferries and water taxis and staffed from early June through Labor Day by trained island managers. (George's Island is accessible from early April through early October.) Guided walks, rest rooms, and first aid are provided on all, but fresh water is available only on Thompson. Food and soft drinks can be purchased only on George's, Thompson, and Peddocks, and lunch and drinks can be purchased on the cruise boats and ferries to George's and Peddocks islands. **Camping** facilities (some with cook stoves) are available on several islands. They are free if regulated by the DEM. A minimal fee is charged for MDC sites. Permits are required, and strict regulations are enforced by both. The chart on page 78 lists facilities and activities available on each island.

If treetop solitude on George's Island is not the thing for you, you can hop aboard a water taxi for Gallops, Lovell's, Bumpkin, Grape, or Peddocks.

Several ferries and cruise boats make frequent daily trips to **George's Island** from the Boston Harbor area from mid-May through October. From George's you can take a water taxi (free) to Gallops, Lovell's, Bumpkin, Grape, or Peddocks. **The Friends of Boston Harbor Islands,** a local volunteer organization dedicated to supplementing and promoting the services of BHI State Park, offer many additional tours, some to islands not serviced by public ferry.

The following islands are accessible by public ferry, water taxi, or, in some cases, bridges and causeways.

Bumpkin Island

Bumpkin is a pretty thirty-five-acre island with flower-strewn paths leading to the stone ruins of a former children's hospital. It's nice to hear the shouts and laughter of healthy children enjoying this pleasant picnic, swimming, fishing, and camping area with their families. During World War I more than thirteen hundred sailors were stationed here in fifty-eight buildings, but little remains of that period except a few foundations. During the summer the water taxi from George's makes one daily trip to Bumpkin on weekdays and several on weekends.

Castle Island

Castle Island, the most accessible and one of the most visited islands, has been linked by bridge, causeway, and landfill to Boston since 1891. The famous short story by Edgar Allan Poe, "The Cask

The famous short story by Edgar Allan Poe, "The Cask of Amontillado," was based on a true incident that happened here in the early 1800s.

of Amontillado," was based on a true incident that happened here in the early 1800s.

Poe was only eighteen years old when he enlisted in the Army and was stationed on Castle Island in 1827. He was immediately impressed with a story he heard of an incident that had occurred at the fort only ten years before. On Christmas Day in 1817 two officers fought a duel over a dispute about a card game. One of the men, a young lieutenant, Robert Massie, was killed in the duel, and his friends decided to avenge his death. They proceeded to get the killer drunk and then led him to a small chamber in the deepest part of the fort's dungeons. After shackling him to the floor, they sealed the entrance to the room and left him there to die. In 1905, when some workmen were renovating the fort and knocked down the wall to a small room, they found a skeleton still dressed in the remnants of an old military uniform. Poe changed the setting of his very similar story to the catacombs of an Italian wine cellar.

The major attraction on Castle Island today is Fort Independence, the oldest continuously used military fortification in the United States. Scheduled tours of the fort are available.

Gallops Island

It's been rumored that a crafty old sea pirate, "Long Ben" Avery, buried a valuable pile of diamonds here, one reported to be the mate of the famous Orloff diamond.

Gallops Island offers some wonderful views of the Boston skyline and surrounding islands from a high, grassy knoll, once the site of a fine resort hotel and restaurant. Nothing remains of the establishment but some old stone foundations. A small sandy beach and huge mussel-shell heaps provide nesting grounds for the island's many gulls. This is a great place to hike, picnic, or try out your treasure-hunting skills. It's been rumored that a crafty old sea pirate, "Long Ben" Avery, buried a valuable pile of diamonds here, one reported to be the mate of the famous Orloff diamond. They've never been found! The water taxi to Gallops leaves George's at frequent intervals and takes only fifteen minutes.

George's Island

This is the site of Fort Warren, a well-preserved granite fort built before the Civil War. During the summer guided tours and special events make this a popular day trip. Also, water taxis to many of the smaller islands depart from here. A schedule of departures is posted near the dock. Other island features include an information booth; a small concession stand that sells food, drinks, and souvenirs; and a pier from which you can fish.

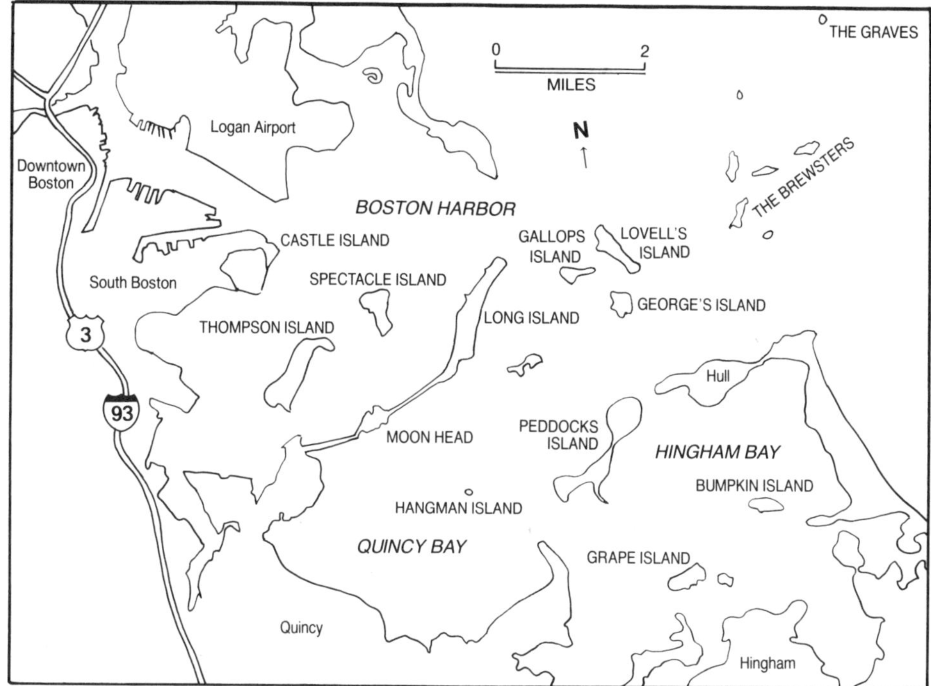

The Boston Harbor Islands

Grape Island

Sorry, there are no longer any grapes on this fifty-acre island, but you can pick the delicious blackberries and raspberries that grow in profusion along the many walking and jogging trails. Captain Smith, alias Amos Pendleton, notorious hermit, one-time slave runner, and smuggler, held sway here for many years following the Civil War. He liked to take pot shots at anyone who dared to come to *his* island. Now you can enjoy the small gravel beach and the quiet fields without fear. The island is about forty minutes from George's by water taxi. One daily trip is made during the week, and several trips are made on weekends.

Long Island

From both land and sea, Long Island is a widely known landmark, with its long causeway and bridge connecting it to the city and its prominent light tower visible for miles around. Another dominant feature of the island is a series of long, rambling buildings that make up the **Long Island Chronic Disease Hospital.** Since 1882 the island has served at one time or another as a refuge for homeless men, paupers, unwed mothers, and alcoholics. A large cemetery on the southern end of the island, with its two thousand unmarked graves, is a grim testimony to the island's past.

In spite of these sad reminders, natural beauty abounds on Long Island. A flourishing wildlife population, including many species of birds, thrives in the marshes and pine woods. Stony beaches offer possibilities for beachcombing, and swimming is best in a small cove on the southeast side of the island. You can still explore the crumbling remains of the old bunkers and batteries of Fort Strong, which was moved to the island just after the Civil War and served as a fortification and campsite for soldiers from 1867 until the end of World War II.

The Woman in Scarlet, one of the many legendary ghosts said to inhabit the Boston Harbor Islands, supposedly dwells on Long Island.

The **Woman in Scarlet,** one of the many legendary ghosts said to inhabit the Boston Harbor Islands, supposedly dwells on Long Island. During the Revolutionary War, as a British ship was preparing to flee Boston Harbor, it was bombarded by American soldiers based on nearby Long Island. One of the passengers, Mary Burton, was mortally struck by a cannonball. Just before she died, she pleaded with her husband not to be buried at sea. A short truce was called so that Mr. Burton could bring his wife ashore for burial on the island. In lieu of using a coffin, her body was sewn into a red blanket and lowered into a small grave. On several occasions since then, various people claim to have seen the form of a woman wearing a scarlet cloak roaming the island and emitting a mournful cry.

Lovell's Island

Here's another island famed for a story of buried treasure, as some gold coins were once found along the beach. These came from the wreck of the ***Magnifique,*** a French man-of-war that sank offshore in 1782. The wreck of the *Magnifique* was blamed on the carelessness of a Boston pilot, David Darling, and the American government, feeling obliged to compensate the French for the loss of this expensive vessel, gave them a new seventy-four-gun ship, the *America*. This ship had been promised to John Paul Jones, an American naval hero, who upon hearing of the transaction, resigned from the Navy forever.

The remains of **Fort Standish,** built in 1900, are found on this sixty-two-acre island, along with several trails, swimming and fishing locations, and a number of good campsites.

Billy-Jean, the island caretaker's pet goat, is not *among the regular sightseeing attractions on Peddocks.*

Peddocks Island

Peddocks has the look and feel of a small community. It boasts several small cottages occupied by summer residents, a church, and guided tours of the

Camping is one attraction on Peddocks, the most densely forested of the Boston Harbor Islands.

decaying remains of **Fort Andrews,** built in 1900. The island, which encompasses 185 acres, is the most densely forested of the Boston Harbor Islands. Plants from all over the world, carried here many years ago in sheep's wool or washed up from shipwrecks, now grow profusely. Many interesting birds also nest here, including the rare black-crowned heron.

An amazing discovery was made on the island in 1971, when a human skeleton was unearthed in a summer resident's backyard. It has been carbon dated at more than four thousand years old, the oldest skeleton ever found in New England. An all-day trip to Peddocks leaves directly from Long Wharf in Boston, and on weekends the water taxi makes one or two trips a day.

Thompson Island

This is one of the most beautifully preserved of the Boston Harbor Islands. It has a long history as an educational center, starting with a school for indigent boys in 1833, which eventually developed into the well-respected **Thompson Academy.** The school was the site of the first vocational education program and the first school band in the nation. In 1975 the island became **Thompson Island Education Center,** a unique education and conference facility. It has residence halls for one hundred fifty, an auditorium, and a gymnasium, and it conducts programs for schoolchildren as well as corporate executives. The 157-acre island is owned and managed by an independent nonprofit trust and is open on a limited basis for guided tours, hiking, and picnicking. Several groups, such as the Boston, Cambridge, and Brookline centers for adult education and the Friends of Boston Harbor Islands, make frequent nature-study and recreational trips to the island.

ACCESS

BOSTON HARBOR. Directions: From north or south I-93 take the Dock Square exit to the Boston waterfront. You will find several parking garages, the closest to the ferries being the aquarium garage. The MBTA Blue Line (subway) stops at the aquarium as well.

CASTLE ISLAND. Directions: The island is an easy drive from downtown Boston. Take exit 17 (South Boston/Dorchester) off the Southeast Expressway. Turn left onto Columbia Road to the rotary and take a right onto Day Boulevard. Follow the shoreline out to the fort. By MBTA, take the City Point bus from Broadway, South Station, or Dudley Station.

GEORGE'S ISLAND. Directions: Several ferry and cruise boats frequently make the 45-minute trip to George's. All are in the area of the New England Aquarium on the waterfront. For information call the following:

Boston Harbor Cruises (617) 227-4321
Bay State Cruises (617) 723-7800
Massachusetts Bay Lines (617) 542-8000.

Ferries to George's Island also leave from Hewett's Cove in Hingham (617) 749-4500, Nantasket Pier in Hull (617) 723-7800, Harbor Light Restaurant in Dorchester (617) 479-3575, and the public landing in Lynn (617) 598-0260. **Season:** Mid-May through October. **Admission:** Charged. **Note:** From George's Island you can take a free water taxi to Gallops, Lovell's, Bumpkin, Grape, and Peddocks islands.

LONG ISLAND. Directions: From Boston take the Southeast Expressway to the Neponset Bridge. Take the first left onto East Squantum Street and follow this directly to the Long Island Bridge. A security guard is posted at the entrance to the island, and permission to enter should be obtained ahead of time by calling (617) 328-1371.

THOMPSON ISLAND. Directions: Take the *Pilgrim IV* from Long Wharf in Boston Harbor (behind the Chart House). **Season:** Year-round. **Admission:** Charged. **Telephone:** (617) 328-3900.

THE FRIENDS OF BOSTON HARBOR ISLANDS. For further information about trips to the islands, write to 20 Parmenter Street, Boston, MA 02113, or call (617) 868-6362.

CAMPING INFORMATION. For a brochure, write to Division of Forests and Parks, Department of Environmental Management, 100 Cambridge Street, Boston, MA 02202, or call (617) 727-3180.

Plum Island

New England skiers are getting used to the idea of ski resorts limiting the sale of lift tickets as a measure of crowd control. But limiting the number of people who can sunbathe on a spacious public beach? Unheard of? Not in Massachusetts.

One of the most beautiful beaches in Massachusetts — which also happens to be one of the best surfcasting spots in New England — is, by design, the least crowded. This despite the fact that it is on an island easily accessible by crossing a small drawbridge by foot, bike, or car.

The explanation is that two-thirds of Plum Island is the **Parker River National Wildlife Refuge**, a salt marsh that provides an important feeding, resting, and nesting area for migratory waterfowl in the Atlantic Flyway. To protect the fragile environment for the abundant wildlife of the refuge, strict regulations limit the number of people who can visit the area at any one time.

If it's sand you're looking for, you won't be disappointed on Plum Island, a natural barrier beach-dune complex.

Plum Island, an area of approximately sixty-five hundred acres located thirty-five miles north of Boston, is one of the few natural barrier beach-dune complexes left in the Northeast. Six miles of heavily vegetated dunes, some as high as fifty feet, parallel the beach, shielding the bays and estuaries from the pounding sea and thus providing a safe haven for wildlife. The southern two-thirds of the island compose the refuge, while the other third is a congested area of small cottages, souvenir shops, fast-food restaurants, and parking lots. The contrast between the two sections of the island is, to say the least, striking.

A causeway from the town of **Newburyport** (an interesting side trip in itself) leads to Plum Island and the refuge. If you are determined enough to get there early (before 9 A.M. from mid-June through August), your car will be one of the three hundred fifty allowed free entrance to the refuge and permitted to drive along the four-mile road to the southern tip of the island. There are several small parking lots (no charge) along the way, and at each you'll find either wooden boardwalks leading through the dunes to the beach or well-trodden trails bordered by scrub pine, willows, beach plum, and wild roses. (There's also a lot of poison ivy, so keep to the paths.) Late-comers have to park outside the refuge at the public beach parking lot and then walk the half-mile to the refuge entrance. If

If you are determined to get there early, your car will be one of the three hundred fifty allowed free entrance to the refuge.

you arrive by auto in the late afternoon (3 P.M.), you usually can get in.

Hellcat Swamp Nature Trail, a two-mile walk skirting a freshwater swamp right in the middle of a bushy sand-dune area, comes complete with a step-by-step printed guide (pick one up at the gate). The guide, which points out such things as beaver trails, borings made in cedar trees by yellow-bellied sapsuckers, and woodchuck burrowing mounds, offers a wonderful way to introduce children to nature study.

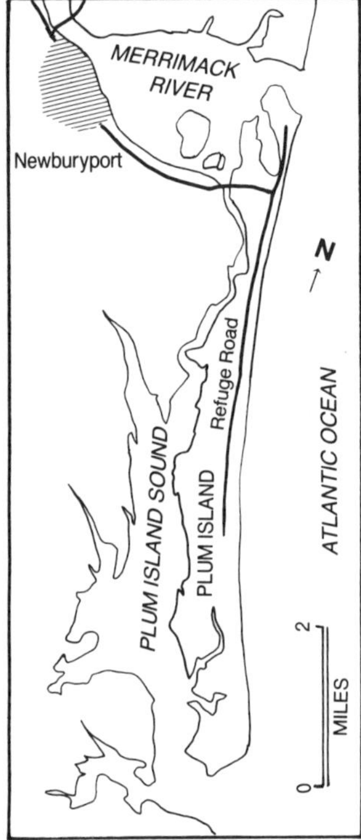

Plum Island

Surf fishing is permitted both day and night on most of the refuge beach, and record numbers of large striped bass have been reeled in here. The bass begin migrating from southern waters in early spring, arriving in the North Atlantic sometime in mid-May. The season lasts throughout the summer until late October. Special permits (obtainable at the refuge center) are necessary for night fishing, which is particularly popular with local fishermen.

The freshwater and saltwater marshes attract thousands of ducks and geese during fall and spring migrations. The refuge is a nesting area from early April through late June, and as many as three hundred species of birds have been sighted here throughout the year. Birders can pick up a list of the birds seen on the refuge at the refuge headquarters, on the northern tip of the island.

The refuge is open all year, and something is going on here all the time. Soon after Labor Day, as the salt marsh begins to blaze with fall colors, you can pick cranberries and beach plums by the bucket. The waterfowl hunting season, which begins in early October, includes a **Youth Waterfowl Hunter Training Program.** Winter songbirds arrive in December, making cross-country skiing a delight.

Be sure to bring along your bike or rent one on the causeway. The refuge is almost never closed to bikers, and if you miss the cutoff for car admittance, a two-wheeler will come in handy. The four-mile road traveling the length of the refuge is partly blacktop and partly hard-packed gravel. Another blacktop road leads from the refuge through the small, densely populated cottage area, with several fast-food restaurants and bait shacks, to the northern tip of the island, where you'll find a lighthouse, the refuge headquarters, and a small fishing dock. **Captain's Fishing Party**, a little store at the dock, sells and rents fishing equipment and charters boats, including the seventy-six-foot *Captain's Lady*, for deep-sea fishing and whale watching. The store also sells gifts and refreshments. Night surf fishing, a favorite sport on the island, is allowed with a license. A license also is needed for clamming.

A unique way to get a bird's-eye view of the island and surrounding areas is to take a short flight aboard an **Air Plum Island** Piper Cub. The flying tours depart from Plum Island Airport, located on Water Street leading out to the island. Weekend tours depart whenever a party of three (or fewer) shows up. The flight circles over the island or follows the coastline for a short distance, with the pilot pointing out landmarks below. The airport has been in existence since 1909, and you're likely to see all sorts of interesting aircraft, from World War II military planes to ultralights.

Soon after Labor Day, as the salt marsh begins to blaze with fall colors, you can pick cranberries and beach plums by the bucket.

You should know a couple of negative things before leaving for Plum Island. First, and worst, is the "greenhead season." For about two weeks during July or August, the island swarms with nasty greenhead flies. You can call refuge headquarters before your trip to get an idea of how bad the situation is. Also, swimmers should know that there is a very strong undertow. If you are bringing along children, it is best to stay in the beach area nearest to the first parking lot, where a lifeguard is on duty.

ACCESS

PLUM ISLAND. Directions: Follow I-95 north to exit marked Route 113 east, Newburyport. This leads you onto Water Street, which becomes Plum Island Turnpike. Take a right onto Sunset Boulevard, and the entrance to the refuge is about a quarter of a mile away.

PARKER RIVER NATIONAL WILDLIFE REFUGE. Directions: After crossing the drawbridge on Plum Island Turnpike, take the first right to the entrance gate. **Season:** Year-round. **Admission:** Free. **Telephone:** (617) 465-5753. **Note:** No more than 350 cars are admitted at one time.

CAPTAIN'S FISHING PARTY. Directions: After crossing the drawbridge on Plum Island Turnpike, take the second left onto Northern Boulevard and follow the road to its end. Captain's is on the right. **Season:** May through September. **Admission:** Charged. **Telephone:** (617) 465-7733 or 462-3141.

AIR PLUM ISLAND. Directions: From Newburyport, take Water Street, following signs to Plum Island and the airport. **Season:** Year-round. **Admission:** Charged. **Telephone:** (617) 462-2114.

NEWBURYPORT CHAMBER OF COMMERCE. 29 State Street, Newburyport, MA 01953; (617) 462-6680.

NEW HAMPSHIRE

Star Island's "comfortable but not modern" Oceanic Hotel provides running water and flush toilets, but generally limits showers to one per person per week.

New Hampshire has the shortest coastline of all the New England states — only eighteen miles long — and only one small group of islands to call its own, the Isles of Shoals. Of the nine islands, none is more than a mile long, and only four actually belong to New Hampshire, with the other five belonging to Maine.

In the early seventeenth century, when prosperous little fishing villages were located on three of the larger islands, all nine were owned by two wealthy Englishmen. In 1635 the men drew a boundary, dividing the islands between themselves, and that boundary has remained unchanged ever since.

The city of **Portsmouth,** which occupies a strategic place on the New Hampshire coastline at the mouth of the Piscataqua (pis-CAT-a-qua) River, has long been an important seaport. It is also the site of the great **Portsmouth Naval Shipyard,** which was actually built on two harbor islands that were joined by bridge and landfill.

Portsmouth is the oldest community in New Hampshire, and early settlers called it **Strawbery Banke** because of the profusion of wild strawberries growing along the river banks. Today the oldest part of the town is still called Strawbery Banke, and a major restoration and rehabilitation project has developed here. Many fine old homes have been restored and are open for touring.

The harbor area of Portsmouth, where many interesting brick buildings had fallen into disuse and disrepair, has been restored as well. Now excellent restaurants and small craft shops are located in these former warehouses. A variety of accommodations is available, from modern motels to old-fashioned inns and several very good bed and breakfast establishments, in case you decide that a stay in Portsmouth is in order following your visit to the islands.

Isles of Shoals

So taken was the inveterate explorer Captain John Smith with the Isles of Shoals that he wrote in his journals in 1616, "... of all foure parts of the world that I have seene not inhabited, could I have but the means to transport a Colonie, I would rather live here then any where ...."

Although he named them Smith's Isles at that time, in hopes of returning, he never did, and this little group of nine islands (eight at low tide when White and Seavey become one island) lying ten miles out from Portsmouth reverted back to their original name, the Isles of Shoals. The name was given to them by fishermen, who trolled the bountiful waters off the islands as early as the 1500s. So plentiful were the cod here that they "shoaled" like bait fish, thus giving the islands their name.

So plentiful were the cod here that they "shoaled" like bait fish, thus giving the islands their name.

According to town records, the fishermen who settled here were a rugged, churlish group with a strong aversion to women. As early as 1635 a court order forbade women to live on the islands. But some of the men eventually married, and the women who did venture out proved to be a feisty bunch

From 1665 the records read, "Joane Forde, wife of Stephen Forde of the Isles of Shoals, given nine stripes for calling the constable a Hornheaded rogue."

themselves. From 1665 the records read, "Joane Forde, wife of Stephen Forde of the Isles of Shoals, given nine stripes for calling the constable a Hornheaded rogue."

The invisible Maine–New Hampshire border runs through the middle of this windswept cluster of rocky isles, giving Duck, Appledore, Malaga, Smuttynose, and Cedar to Maine, and Star, Lunging, White, and Seavey to New Hampshire. But as Portsmouth is the nearest mainland access and communication link to the islands, and the dominant center of activity is Star Island, the entire group is usually regarded as part of the Granite State.

As with so many of New England's islands, after the fishing industry died out a new spirit of activity was created by the brief era of the summer resort. The Isles of Shoals gained tremendous popularity, and what set them apart from similar island communities was their attraction for some of the more illustrious literary personalities of the day.

Celia Thaxter, who grew up on the islands and is closely identified with them, became one of the leading woman poets of her day — on an island that once forbade women! Her father, Thomas Leighton, an entrepreneur and former importer, editor, and politician, moved his family to the islands and built a hotel on Appledore in 1848. The Appledore Hotel, one of the first island resorts in the area, became the summer choice of such leading New England writers and artists as Nathaniel Hawthorne, Ralph Waldo Emerson, James Russell Lowell, John Greenleaf Whittier, Mark Twain, Lucy Larcome, Childe Hassam, and Sarah Orne Jewett. Hawthorne delighted in the unusually long "piazza or promenade . . . so situated that the breeze draws across it from the sea on one side of the island to the sea on the other, and it is the breeziest and comfortablest place in the whole world on a hot day."

Thaxter's writings about the islands often were filled with sadness and longing, because in later

The Isles of Shoals

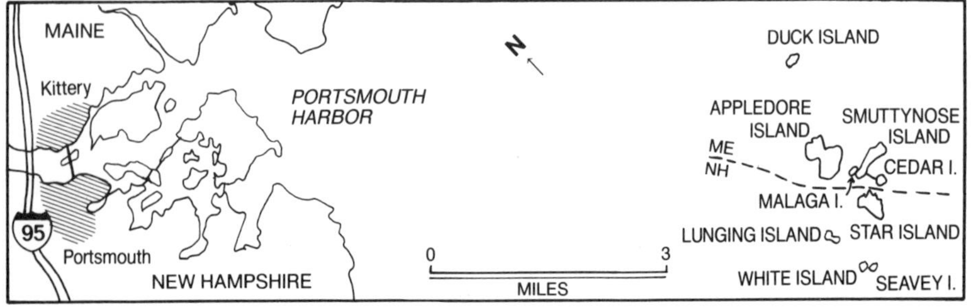

The chapel and other buildings on Star Island are built of native stone.

years her marriage made it difficult for her to return to them as often as she would have liked. She wrote, "Landing for the first time the stranger is struck only by the sadness of the place, — the vast loneliness; for there are not even trees to whisper with familiar voices, — nothing but sky and sea and rocks. But the very wildness and desolation reveal a strange beauty. . . ." The beauty of which she speaks is wonderfully revealed in the bright Impressionism of artist Childe Hassam. Several of his paintings, including the renowned *The South Ledges of Appledore,* hang in the National Museum of American Art in Washington, D.C.

Appledore, named in 1661 by English settlers for a hamlet off the coast of Devon, England, is the largest island of the group, yet it is less than a mile in length and width. It now includes the **Shoals Marine Laboratory**, a field station where undergraduates interested in marine science can further their studies during the summer. It is operated jointly by Cornell University and the University of New Hampshire, and credit and noncredit courses covering all areas of marine biology are open to the public. You can choose, for example, a five-day "Sea Floor to Table" seminar, which culminates with a banquet of freshly caught seafood prepared by participants under the guidance of an island chef. Or how about a five-day course in nature photography drawing on the island's wealth of subjects — seabird colonies, wildflowers, and the diverse marine life. There are also courses in marine biology specifically for teachers, and certified divers with a scientific background can enroll in a special course in underwater research. The price of these courses, including full tuition, room, board, all field trips, and round-trip ferry charges, is around five hundred dollars per person.

But when it comes to out-of-the-ordinary vacations, probably nothing surpasses "Life on a Star" — **Star Island Conferences**. In 1915, when Star Island came up for sale, it was bought by a group of Congregationalists and Unitarians who formed the Star Island Corporation. Since that time, week-long conferences have been held on the island throughout the summer for families, young adults, religious educators, and just about anyone interested in topics such as the arts, natural history, religion, or international affairs. The conferences are very relaxed, and while they may not always inspire religious and educational thought, as is their intent, they never fail to create a warm spirit of community. Some wonderful traditions are observed at the conferences, including the silent trek up to the chapel each evening, with everyone carrying a lighted lantern. At the conclusion of each weekly conference, staff members bid farewell to "shoalers" (the name given to conference attendants) at the dock with the chant, "You *will* come back; you *will* come back."

The conferences are very relaxed, and while they may not always inspire religious and educational thought, as is their intent, they never fail to create a warm spirit of community.

The conferences are particularly fun for families. While adults attend their various activities, children participate in their own special program, supervised by a creative professional staff. Activities include classes in nature study and marine biology through walks and explorations of the natural surroundings, art, music, and organized sports. Child care for children under three years of age is provided during the day, and an evening babysitting service is available at reasonable rates.

Everyone eats together in the large dining room of the old **Oceanic Hotel,** and a group of college-age people, called Pelicans, serve the meal. To be a Pelican on Star Island has long been the aspiration of many young conference attendants. In fact, quite often there is a waiting list for the job.

Children have a wonderful time on Star Island; it's just the right size for exploring. And what great places to discover! There's the **Lemon Squeeze** and the **Orange Squeeze,** slender rock crevices just big enough for little bodies to squiggle through. And don't miss **Betty Moody's Cave**, with its sad story of a mother who accidentally smothered her crying child while hiding there during an Indian raid. Legends of pirates and buried treasure come alive in the story of **Haley's Breakwater,** built in 1820 with the proceeds from actual pirate treasure — four bars of silver dug up on Smuttynose by Captain Samuel Haley.

It is possible to visit Star Island or Appledore for the day by taking the ***Viking*** out of Portsmouth. The daily cruise boat leaves Portsmouth at mid-morning and returns at mid-afternoon. You have about three hours on the island, including a guided tour. A staff member from the Shoals Marine Laboratory on Appledore usually meets the morning boat from Portsmouth at the Star Island dock and takes interested passengers by free water taxi to Appledore for a tour. It is always best to telephone ahead to let them know you are coming. There is a snack bar at the hotel on Star (the dining room is for conference members only), or you can buy food aboard the *Viking* for a picnic on the island.

Hotel accommodations are for conference members only, and no camping is allowed on any of the islands. Star and Appledore are the only two islands open to the public. Except for a few fishing cottages, the smaller islands are almost entirely nesting areas for several kinds of shore and marine birds, which strongly object to visitors. The gulls, even on Star and Appledore, can be quite aggressive, screaming and diving at you if you get too close to their nests.

"Shoalers" bid departing visitors the traditional farewell, chanting "You will *come back; you* will *come back."*

ACCESS

PORTSMOUTH. Directions: Take I-95 (New Hampshire Turnpike) exit 7 to downtown Portsmouth.

***VIKING* CRUISES. Directions:** Turn right off exit 7 of I-95 onto Market Street. The *Viking*'s dock is about one mile along on the left. **Season:** Mid-June through Labor Day. **Admission:** Charged. **Telephone:** (603) 431-5500.

SHOALS MARINE LABORATORY. G-14-A, Stimson Hall, Cornell University, Ithaca, NY 14853; (607) 256-3717.

STAR ISLAND CONFERENCES. Star Island Corporation, 110 Arlington Street, Boston, MA 02116; (617) 426-7988.

PORTSMOUTH CHAMBER OF COMMERCE. P.O. Box 239, Portsmouth, NH 03801; (603) 436-1118.

MAINE

These stilt-supported houses and fishing shacks in Matinicus Harbor stand ready for the proverbial high water.

Geologists call the coast of Maine a "drowned coastline." As the huge ice cap from the north began to melt and recede in this area, the ocean rose and water surged across what was once a high range of coastal mountains. To the naked eye, all that remains of these mountains today are their now rounded and smoothed peaks, poking through the surface of the vast sea, creating literally thousands of islands. The state of Maine's very name derives from having to distinguish the "mainland" from its many offshore islands.

Also left behind by the retreating glacier was an irregular coastline of twenty-five hundred miles (half of the United States' Atlantic coastline). Not all of it is merely "rock-bound," as the saying goes, for there are miles and miles of sandy beaches, areas of marshy lowlands, and great stands of hemlock, spruce, and fir.

No one knows for sure just how many islands are off the coast of Maine, but the number has been estimated at well over three thousand. Only about half of them are considered inhabitable, and most of these are privately owned. Fewer than a dozen have year-round communities, and the number of residents on these ranges from around fifty on Frenchboro to well over a thousand on Vinalhaven. But as the summer season approaches, the population on all the islands more than doubles; in the case of Monhegan, it increases tenfold!

Some of the oldest settlements in the country were started on these islands. French, English, Spanish, and Dutch explorers sailed among the islands, often giving them such exotic names as Malaga, Placentia, and Bois Bubert. But more often than not, the islands were named for their chief inhabitants: Sheep, Horse, Goat, Hog, Cow, and even Brown Cow. Such animals were pastured here, where they were safe from thieves and wolves.

The problem with such names is that they cause a great deal of confusion. As it turns out there are about thirteen Sheep islands, at least ten Cow islands, innumerable Hog islands (although for obvious reasons, some of the owners have changed the islands' names), and dozens of other animals in various quantities. The same dilemma holds true for islands named for their shapes. You'll find more than fifteen Bar or Barred islands, plenty of Round, Little, Small, Big, and High islands, at least two Crotch islands (although the owners of one have changed its name to Cliff), and more Long islands than you can shake a stick at. You'll also find a White, Black, and Green island in almost every bay.

Some islands were named for the method of barter their owners used to acquire them, such as Pound of Tea or Junk of Pork. Then again, there is no accounting for names such as The Shivers, Bum Key, Bombazeen, The Cuckholds, Eastern Ear, Hamloaf, Despair, Old Woman, Lazygut, and Drunkard Ledge. Thrumcap is a very popular island name, and Maine has at least six of them. Early weavers used the ends of warp threads, called thrums, to make small caps; hence any small island shaped like a cap was called Thrumcap.

The Maine islands discussed in this book are accessible by public ferry or, in some cases, by

Along the deserted beaches and in the quiet woods on a clear spring day, after the silver fog has lifted, you feel like the sole inhabitant on a deserted island.

bridge or causeway. All of them welcome visitors, some more than others. While most Maine islands are predominantly small fishing communities, tourism helps to balance the economies of many.

Summer, of course, is the prime time to visit the islands, but many travelers prefer to go off-season (September through May). Seeing the islands' flora and fauna spring to life in April and May can be inspiring. Along the deserted beaches and in the quiet woods on a clear spring day, after the silver fog has lifted, you feel like the sole inhabitant on a deserted island.

Many of the islands remain accessible to visitors throughout the fall for bird watching, hunting, and horseback riding. Clear, crisp days make autumn a great time for camping and cooking over a driftwood fire, and you have the added advantage of New England's spectacular fall foliage. Even winter has something special to offer: scenic paths for cross-country skiing and frozen ponds of "black ice" for skating and fishing.

Both the Maine State Ferry Service and mail boats run year-round to the islands, although their schedules are significantly reduced in the winter months. Passenger rates vary. State ferries are the least expensive, with costs being determined by the length of the trip. Prices range from less than three dollars to as much as twenty dollars. While a few of the mail boat charges are fairly inexpensive (less than three dollars), most are in the ten-dollar range for a round trip, and some cost more.

CASCO BAY

Casco Bay is truly a delightful place for island hopping. Here, shimmering like jewels in the noonday sun or draped in lacy fog on a misty morning, are well over a hundred islands: tiny, remote, deserted ones with mysterious little harbors and strange names such as Bombazeen and Uncle Zeek; and "big" ones such as fashionable Great Chebeague (two and a half by five miles) and bustling Peaks.

The bay begins at Portsmouth, New Hampshire, and spreads northeasterly for a distance of about twenty miles. It is twelve miles across at its widest. As seen from the window of a small, low-flying plane, the Casco Bay islands are especially tantalizing, appearing only a skip and a jump from one another. While a few actually are almost connected at low tide, you must be a pretty strong

All greased up and no place to go? Swimmers prepare for the annual Peaks-to-Portland Maine Race.

swimmer to make it from one to another without a boat. The challenge of swimming from one island to another has been braved over the years — both successfully and unsuccessfully — and the recently revived 2.5-mile **Peaks-to-Portland (Maine) Race** has become a popular event each August.

You may have heard the term "Calendar Islands." Well, it originated here. If you ask New Englanders who live on large bays or lakes how many islands there are, they'll usually answer, "One for every day of the year. That's why we call them the Calendar Islands." The name is used more often in connection with Casco Bay than with any other area because some early explorer called them that. In fact, the number of islands in these waters is somewhere around 135 at high tide, more than are found in any similar body of water in the United States.

The number of islands in these waters is somewhere around 135 at high tide, more than are found in any similar body of water in the United States.

The name Casco Bay comes from a sixteenth-century explorer, Esteban Gomez, who named it Bahia de Casco, which means the Bay of the Helmet or Skull. These islands, explored by Vikings probably around A.D. 1000 and used as fishing and hunting grounds by the Abnaki Indians for no one knows how long, were settled by Europeans long before these same colonists built towns on the "maine." They've had a long and colorful history, and stories — some less fact than fancy — of famous pirates, shipwrecks, resorts, industries, ghosts, and notorious criminals abound.

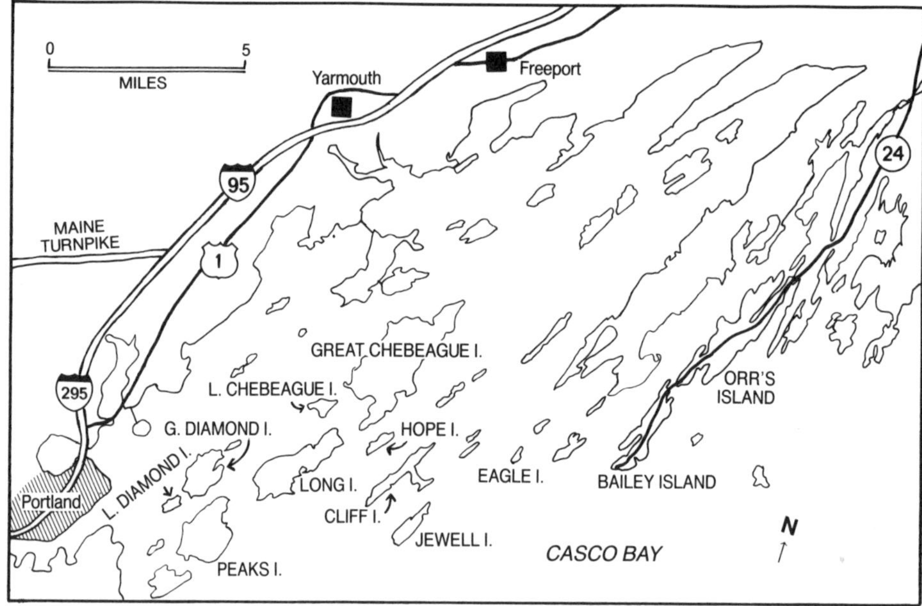

Casco Bay Islands

A good way to get an overall view of the islands is to take one of the numerous boat trips, cruises, and ferries out of Portland harbor. You can choose from narrated inner and outer bay cruises, sunset and moonlight cruises, and special trips to **Bailey Island** for a lobster dinner (freshly caught) or to **Eagle Island** to visit the former home of North Pole discoverer Admiral Robert E. Peary and to picnic on the wide front lawn.

Long Island is known for its beautiful beaches, and many people like to go out on an early ferry to spend the day at **Andrews or Singing Beach**, and then take the late-afternoon ferry back to Portland. **Cliff Island** is a small, private summer colony where the casual visitor can stop for a few hours, walk down the quiet scenic roads, and have a light lunch at the village restaurant before catching the ferry to the mainland. **House Island,** close to Portland, also is privately owned, but the owner schedules daily boat trips (summer only) out to the island for groups to enjoy a lobster cookout and a tour of the remnants of a Civil War–era fort located there. While **Jewell Island** is accessible only by private boat, the Maine Audubon Society takes group trips there several times a year for bird watching and observations of nature and marine life.

The city of **Portland** itself is full of history — more than three hundred fifty years of it — and there are many interesting places to visit there as well. The **Wadsworth-Longfellow House,** boyhood home of the American poet, and the **Portland Museum of Art,** with its permanent collection of works by Winslow Homer and Andrew Wyeth, are both well worth seeing. Many fine restaurants and overnight accommodations are available, and the **Old Port Exchange** district is filled with craft shops, boutiques, and cafes.

While many of the islands of Casco Bay are privately owned, more than enough are open for the explorer to investigate. Most of the islands included in this chapter have frequent and reliable ferry service for most or all of the year. While some of the islands mentioned have ferry service only during the summer months or not at all, it is still possible to visit them throughout the year on field trips arranged by organizations such as the Maine Audubon Society and the Maine chapter of The Nature Conservancy.

ACCESS

PORTLAND. Directions: Take exit 6A off I-95 to I-295. From I-295 take Route 1 north then Route 1A, which becomes Commercial Street, following "Waterfront" signs to the wharves, where various ferries and cruise boats dock.

CHAMBER OF COMMERCE OF THE GREATER PORTLAND REGION. 142 Free Street, Portland, ME 04104; (207) 772-2811.

Little and Great Chebeague Islands

There are two Chebeagues — Little and Great — but only Great Chebeague has facilities for visitors. Little Chebeague, about half a mile long, has a nice beach and is now part of the Maine state park system. At low tide, a sandspit (sandbar) connects the two islands, and you can walk from Great Chebeague to Little Chebeague to enjoy the beach or to explore. There was once a small settlement here, and during World War II the island was occupied by the United States Navy. Few remnants of human habitation remain, however, except for some old stone foundations and occasional patches of garden flowers. Tour guides on the narrated cruises around the islands enjoy telling passengers how, in 1950, the federal government offered the island to the State of Maine and the City of Portland for one dollar. Neither accepted the offer, and Little Che-

Seasoned eyes take in the view of Casco Bay from the deck of a Casco Bay Lines ferry.

PAT MALONE

beague went on the auction block, selling for more than six thousand dollars. After twenty years and the death of the owner, the state bought the island from his heirs in 1972. The price: $155,000.

Great Chebeague (pronounced sha-BEEG) is the largest of the Casco Bay islands and has the flavor and feel of an elegant summer resort. Actually, it has a year-round population of around four hundred, but it has been a popular summer colony for well over a hundred years.

The island's only hotel, the **Chebeague Inn**, is an old-fashioned inn with a huge wraparound porch and big, square waterfront windows. It's perched atop a hill, situated just right to catch the best view of the sunset. A pretty nine-hole golf course, which is open to the public, stretches along the ocean in front of the hotel. Boaters have been known to sail into the harbor early in the afternoon for a round of golf before sitting down to a delicious, freshly caught crab dinner, a specialty of the inn.

Chebeague Islanders unload the daily mailboat.

Tennis courts are located close to the inn, and bicycles are available for guests. The island has about twenty-five miles of winding scenic roads. (Day-trippers should bring their own bikes.) You will find a good beach for cooling off and two grocery stores for purchasing snacks. The dining room at the inn is open to the public and serves breakfast, lunch, and dinner.

Chebeague's history differs somewhat from that of most of the Casco Bay islands, and the difference has to do with the "stone sloops." During the late nineteenth and early twentieth centuries, the islands farther up the coast, such as Vinalhaven and Deer, were producing large quantities of granite to be shipped to the major cities along the East Coast. Ambrose Hamilton of Chebeague built and owned the famous stone sloops, the large sailing ships that transported the heavy granite to its destination, and most of the captains who sailed them were Chebeaguers. Great fortunes were made during this time, and the expression "stone sloop money" came into being. Most of the fine old houses seen on the island today were built with so-called stone sloop money.

At the turn of the century, Chebeague had its share of resort hotels, but never quite as many or as elaborate as those built on other islands. Now it has settled into a peaceful little summer resort, with many descendants of the stone sloop captains still enjoying a quiet summer holiday here.

ACCESS

CASCO BAY LINES. Directions: The ferry leaves about four times a day from Custom House Wharf in Portland. **Season:** Year-round. **Admission:** Charged. **Telephone:** (207) 774-7871.

CHEBEAGUE TRANSPORTATION COMPANY. Directions: A water taxi from Cousins Island (connected to the mainland by a bridge) makes frequent 15-minute trips to Chebeague. Because there is no parking at the dock on Cousins, you have to park several miles away and take the free shuttle bus to the ferry landing. Take I-95 north to exit 9. Follow Route 1 north to the second overpass and turn right onto Tuttle Road. Follow this to Drowne Road (approximately ¼ mile past the railroad crossing). Turn left onto Drowne Road, go to the end, and park in the school yard. The shuttle bus comes every half-hour to take passengers to the ferry landing. **Season:** Year-round. **Admission:** Charged. **Telephone:** (207) 846-3700.

CHEBEAGUE INN. Directions: From the water taxi the inn is just up the hill; from the ferry it is across the island (guests are met at the wharf and taxied to the inn). **Season:** Mid-May to mid-October. **Telephone:** (207) 846-5155.

Eagle Island

In this age of space travel and moon landings, it is sometimes hard to believe that something as earthly as the North Pole also was discovered in this century. A trip to Eagle Island, the **summer home of** the famed explorer **Admiral Robert E. Peary,** brings it all into perspective.

Peary, who graduated from Portland High School and Bowdoin College in Brunswick, Maine, loved this island, and his family lived here for fifty years. While still a young man and an ensign in the U.S. Navy, he managed to save enough money to buy the island. It was to be many years before he could afford to build a house on it, and when he did, the house was made with the island's native rock and wood. It was in this house that Peary drew the plans for his explorations of the North Pole. And it was also here that Mrs. Peary received word from the admiral in September 1909 that he had discovered the North Pole.

Peary's home is a museum, preserved as it was when he lived here, filled with memorabilia from his life on the island and his famous explorations.

Today, the island is owned by the State of Maine and is on the National Register of Historic Landmarks. Peary's home is a museum, preserved as it was when Peary lived here, filled with memorabilia from his life on the island and from his famous explorations. Two huge, round, fortresslike

BUREAU OF PARKS AND RECREATION/ MAINE DEPT. OF CONSERVATION

Admiral Robert E. Peary built this house on Eagle Island in 1904, five years before he discovered the North Pole. The photograph was taken in the 1940s or 1950s.

structures form the base of Peary's home. One of these structures was a cistern built to store up to forty thousand gallons of rainwater. The other, facing north, was Peary's library and workshop, and its porthole windows were salvaged from old ships. A large fieldstone fireplace made from stones gathered on the island and white quartz from the Arctic dominates the living room. Many stuffed and mounted arctic birds, most of which were prepared by Peary himself, are displayed throughout the house.

The seventeen-acre island, which was named for the bald eagles that once nested here, is crisscrossed with nature trails that wind through berry patches and rocky cliffs. The ***Kristy K*** out of Portland makes two trips to the island each day during the summer. You can bring a picnic lunch (there are no food facilities on the island) and enjoy the scenery from the Peary house's wide, sloping front lawn. The cruise aboard the *Kristy K* takes about four hours, stopping at Eagle Island for one hour, then cruising out to Bailey Island, past many of the other islands of Casco Bay. The cruise is narrated, and along the way a lobster pot is usually hauled aboard. A passenger holding a lucky ticket wins the lobster (providing there is one in the trap).

ACCESS

KRISTY K. **Directions:** The boat leaves from Long Wharf, 170 Commercial Street, in Portland. **Season:** Mid-June through Labor Day, weather permitting. **Admission:** Charged. **Telephone:** (207) 774-6498 or 846-9592.

Peaks Island

The ferryboat trip to Peaks Island is one of the shortest you're likely to take. It's less than twenty minutes on any good day out of Portland harbor. The trip is so short, in fact, that Peaks is considered a bedroom community for people working in Portland. The island always has been a popular destination for summer day-trippers, but only in the past decade, with the rapid rise in popularity and the renewal of downtown Portland attracting many new people, has the year-round population of the island soared. There are now about sixteen hundred year-round residents (compared to about a thousand ten years ago), and the number jumps to more than six thousand in the summer — not to mention the hundreds of visitors who come out each sunny day to partake of the island's recreational facilities.

The proximity to Portland and the excellent year-round ferry service — both car and passenger — have made Peaks a most desirable location. "I can walk from my office and catch the 5:30 every night," says a young Portland lawyer, "and then walk to my home on the island. It sure beats bucking highway traffic every day!"

Peaks was not very popular among early white settlers, however. Its nearness to the shore was a great disadvantage in the 1600s, inviting attacks from unfriendly Indians. This had long been a popular Indian summering place, and they didn't take kindly to the new people taking over their land. After a particularly bloody battle in 1689, almost a century passed before a white settlement actually took hold here.

The real heyday of Peaks came in the mid-1800s when an amusement park, a skating rink, a theater, and a number of hotels and boarding houses were built on the island. For a grand total of twenty-five cents, hundreds of day-trippers received steamer passage to the island for a full day's outing, including a theater show. The island was then billed as "The Belle of the Bay," and theatergoers got to enjoy some of the first hits by a producer who later rose to fame on Broadway, George M. Cohan. Some of the brightest stars of both stage and screen came here to play in America's first summer stock theater company.

Some of the brightest stars of both stage and screen came here to play in America's first summer stock theater company.

After several disastrous fires that wiped out many homes and amusements, and the invention of the automobile that took fun-seekers to other places, Peaks' popularity declined sharply. During both world wars military fortifications were built on the backside of the island, which became "off limits" to visitors. More recently, however, a group of islanders formed an association and bought this

On the way down you pass a former control tower that has been made into an interesting summer home, complete with curtains and flower pots.

land back from the government to keep it from being developed. It's open to the public for hiking and picnicking. Many old bunkers, dark tunnels, and observation towers thick with overgrown vines and vegetation still provide some pretty exciting explorations for the adventurous.

The roads leading up to these remains, located at **Tollman Heights,** are steep and rocky and definitely not for biking. Tim Fitzgerald, who summered on the island before moving here permanently several years ago, provides **taxi service** to the site and can give you a good idea of how the gun emplacements and other fortifications worked. "Security was so tight in those days," he says, "that everyone on the island had to have an ID card, along with being fingerprinted." After he recounts some of the intense and scary maneuvers that patrols were put through, you may be glad to leave the scene behind. On the way down you pass a former control tower that has been made into an interesting summer house, complete with curtains and flower pots. It is a curious contrast.

Several sandy beaches and rocky shoreline areas are available for swimming, sunbathing, and fishing. One particularly scenic spot, called **Big Daddy**, is on the backside of the island and is popular for daytime picnics and nighttime parties. A flat, well-paved road circles the island, providing an enjoyable five-mile bike ride. You can rent bikes on the island, but the selection is limited. You might want to rent one at one of the large bicycle rental shops in Portland and bring it over on the ferry.

JOHN EWING

Swimming, fishing, and sunbathing are among the attractions of Peaks Island's several sandy and rocky beaches.

The island has several small restaurants, shops, stores, and even a hair salon called Kinks. **Jones Landing** is the biggest attraction in the harbor area, serving lunch, dinner, and drinks. It's a popular gathering spot for islanders, particularly in the evening, with its wide deck looking out toward the twinkling Portland skyline. Some people come out from the city just to have dinner there and to enjoy the sunset.

Jane MacDermott and her husband run a gift and card shop, **MacDermott's**, on the corner of Island Avenue and the dock road. The store features many craft items made by the local senior citizens group, including knitted sweaters, mittens, doll and bear clothes, quilted items, and some Christmas things. The shop stays open through the Christmas season. "I always keep the coffeepot going when it's cold out," says Jane, "and a lot of people drop by for a visit." Jane says she always wanted a shop of her own and, although living in Portland at the time, didn't hesitate when this one came on the market. "As soon as we heard it was for sale we bought it — and haven't been sorry since. I *love* it here."

Moonshell Inn, a bed and breakfast establishment run by Bunny Clark, is located on the "water side" of Island Avenue. It is just a short walk from the ferry landing and, though small, has large rooms with water views. It's within walking distance of everything — stores, Laundromat, library, and churches — and is open year-round.

Passengers awaiting the ferry back to Portland often find the Harbor Deli a satisfying last stop on the island.

ACCESS

CASCO BAY LINES. Directions: Located at Custom House Wharf, Commercial Street in Portland. The car ferry leaves from Portland Pier, one block west of Custom House Wharf. **Season:** Frequent daily trips year-round. The car ferry does not run on Wednesdays. Peaks Island is usually the first stop on the mail-boat run. **Admission:** Charged. **Telephone:** (207) 774-7871.

PEAKS ISLAND TAXI. Directions: The taxi meets almost every boat from 6 A.M. to 6 P.M. during the summer, but it is best to call ahead and make reservations. **Telephone:** (207) 766-2777.

JONES LANDING. Directions: The restaurant is on the left, just up the hill from the ferry dock. **Season:** Year-round. **Telephone:** (207) 766-5542.

MACDERMOTT'S. Directions: From the ferry landing walk up to Island Avenue. The store is on the left corner. **Season:** April through December. **Telephone:** (207) 766-2755.

MOONSHELL INN. Directions: From the ferry landing walk up to Island Avenue, turn left, and the inn is about two blocks along on the left side of the street (across from the fire station). **Season:** Year-round. **Telephone:** (207) 766-2331.

Bailey and Orr's Islands

Along the eastern side of Casco Bay lies the town of Harpswell, made up of a series of jagged little peninsulas and points and several small islands. Some of the larger islands are now connected to one another and to the mainland by bridges, with Great Island, Orr's, and Bailey being the three most distinguished.

If you drive down the main road of the peninsula (Route 24), crossing Great, Orr's, and Bailey, you'll pass any number of small, picturesque fishing coves, their docks piled high with lobster traps and buoys, attesting to what has been the principal occupation here for ages. You'll also find an equal number of small restaurants serving up the famed crustacean — baked, boiled, broiled, steamed — on plates, in baskets, or just about any way you like. So popular are the Harpswell islands for their lobster that during the summer several boats leave Custom House Wharf in Portland to take passengers over to the islands for sightseeing and a shore dinner.

At Land's End stands this monument "to all Maine fishermen who have devoted their lives to the sea."

If you drive your own car, however, you'll get to cross one of the most unusual bridges in the world. It connects Bailey Island to Orr's (over Will's Gut) and is called a **cribstone bridge.** This structure, measuring 1,150 feet across and built in 1928, is made of huge granite blocks laid honeycomb fashion, which permits the free flow of swift tidal currents, ice floes, and boat traffic. It's the only bridge of its kind in the world and is a National Historic Civil Engineering Landmark.

This area also is known as the place where a number of famous American writers and poets produced some of their important work. Harriet Beecher Stowe, known for her book *Uncle Tom's Cabin,* wrote an early American classic, *The Pearl of Orr's Island,* while summering on Orr's. Robert P. Tristram Coffin, beloved poet and writer of Maine, focused much of his work on this area, and Edna St. Vincent Millay, one of the more popular poets of her era, summered on nearby Ragged Island.

This is also one of the few areas on the New England coast where a tale of discovering buried treasure has been authenticated. In 1840 a local fisherman, John Wilson, slipped on some rocks on Cedar Ledges and fell into a hole. There he discovered a pot of Spanish doubloons worth about twelve thousand dollars at that time.

If you drive to the tip of Bailey Island, called **Land's End,** the views are spectacular. A large, impressive monument erected here, the figure of a local fisherman at work, serves as a tribute "to all Maine fishermen who devote their lives to the sea."

Harpswell is only a short distance from Brunswick (home of **Bowdoin College**) and Bath (location of the **Maine Maritime Museum**), so there are plenty of motels, inns, bed and breakfast establishments, and campgrounds in the area. Several major art and musical events take place throughout the summer on the Bowdoin campus, and nearby **Thomas Point Beach** offers a full schedule of family entertainment, including folk festivals and antique auto shows.

ACCESS

HARPSWELL. Directions: From Route 1 take Route 24 south at Cook's Corner, following signs to the islands.

CASCO BAY LINES. Boat tours leave from Custom House Wharf in Portland twice daily and from Cook's Lobster House on Bailey Island once a day. **Season:** Last weekend in June to Labor Day. **Admission:** Charged. **Telephone:** (207) 774-7871.

Great and Little Diamond

The Diamonds, connected by a sandbar at low tide, probably have the most appropriate names of any of the Casco Bay islands; they are jewels. Family jewels, that is, and they are guarded and protected as such. The Diamonds are private islands, each owned by an association, and casual visitors are discouraged from walking around here. There are no public facilities, no roads, and no public beaches; without an invitation, you quickly feel like a trespasser here.

It was not always thus. For more than two centuries the islands were the sole domain of hogs. In fact, Great Diamond was called Hog Island. The first settlers used the island as a large hog yard where the animals could roam freely without fences and be safe from wolves and dogs.

The early history of the islands is related by the island historian, Hal Hackett, who claims to be a relative "newcomer" to Little Diamond. "I'm only second generation compared to some who have been here five and six generations," he says.

Hal Hackett, Diamond Island historian, describes himself as "only second generation" islander.

"The tenant farming period at Hog Island probably began about 1743," Hackett says, "and the farms provided hay, grain, and vegetable crops as well as pasturage to the town-dwelling owners." By the late 1800s the beauty of both islands was well recognized by their owners, and a summer colony was developed here. A unique feature of the colony, and of the islands today, is that they (particularly Little Diamond) are owned almost exclusively by Portland area people.

The Casino, a handsome shingled structure with a wide front veranda, sits squarely at the entrance to the dock, facing the harbor, and originally served as an attractive seafood restaurant. Eventually it was bought by the Island Association (which owns all the land on the island and maintains the

Walking paths like these are the only "roads" on the Diamonds.

footpaths connecting the cottages), and a long tradition of Saturday night suppers began. "Every Saturday night two or three families in turn prepare dinner for the other islanders," Hackett explains. Each family supplies its own dishes (china — not paper), placemats, and silver.

If you want to visit the Diamonds, plan to attend the **Annual Craft Fair and Lobster Bake** put on by the Sisters of Mercy, who run a small summer camp for children on the east end of Little Diamond. The camp land was given to James Healy, the second Bishop of Portland, in 1882. He built a summer home there for orphans and every summer held a huge picnic. According to Hackett, the annual Bishop's Picnic was "the major social event of Catholic Portland between 1883 and 1900."

Sister Nola Wells now runs a well-attended **Ecology Day Camp** for Portland area children. For three two-week periods children from seven to fourteen years of age come to the island each day on the ferry for "an adventure in ecology suited to the age of the child, related crafts and projects, enrichment activities, baking bread, and playing games."

Camp closes for a week prior to the two-day annual fair so everyone can help with the enormous food preparations for the meals, which include a smorgasbord lunch on Saturday and Sunday and a lobster bake on both evenings. Cakes and lobsters by the hundreds, pounds of beans and potatoes, and gallons of coffee and fruit drinks are prepared.

Camp closes for a week prior to the two-day annual fair so everyone can help with the enormous food preparations for the meals.

The money from this project goes toward restoration of the existing buildings, and Sister Nola hopes it will one day help "to build a badly needed new building." Along with running the camp and helping to prepare all the food, Sister Nola whips up dozens of pounds of her famous fudge to sell at the fair. The fair is usually held during a weekend in August and affords a nice opportunity to visit the otherwise inaccessible Little Diamond Island.

ACCESS

CASCO BAY LINES. Directions: The ferry from Custom House Wharf in Portland makes about six trips each day to Great and Little Diamond. Remember, however, that visitors are generally not welcome here, except at the annual fair. **Season:** Year-round (infrequent stops off-season as requested). **Admission:** Charged. **Telephone:** (207) 774-7871.

SISTERS OF MERCY ECOLOGY DAY CAMP. Sister

Nola Wells, Sisters of Mercy Ecology Day Camp, 242 Walton Street, Portland, ME 04103; (207) 797-4895 or 766-2012.

BOOTHBAY HARBOR ISLANDS

During the summer months, the town of Boothbay Harbor is probably one of the busiest, most congested areas on the entire Maine coast. The streets, choked with traffic, are narrow and one-way and are lined with many alluring shops and restaurants, as well as guesthouses and motels that are filled to capacity. The town is the kind of place people come to from miles around to browse in the shops, feast on seafood dinners, and take boat trips on the numerous sightseeing and deep-sea fishing vessels that jam the harbor.

People come from miles around to browse in the shops, feast on seafood dinners, and take boat trips on the numerous sightseeing and deep-sea fishing vessels that jam the harbor.

A few miles out into the waters off Boothbay Harbor, though, away from all this hustle and bustle, lie several serene islands that manage to retain vestiges of times past. Three of them are particularly interesting: Damariscove, a nature preserve; Squirrel, a quintessential "association" island; and Capitol, one of the biggest bargains left on all the Maine coast.

About four miles southeast of the mainland lies the two-hundred-acre **Damariscove Island.** This is the site of one of the earliest settlements in

Young Squirrel Islanders collect fresh water.

Maine and appears on the National Register of Historic Places. Once a thriving farming community, providing milk and fresh vegetables for the summer inhabitants of nearby Squirrel Island, it is now an important bird sanctuary. Along with a large population of black-backed and herring gulls, it supports one of the largest nesting populations of common eider in the eastern United States.

During the summer months a caretaker lives on the island and will provide information to visitors. Most people come by private boat, but field trips for bird watchers and explorers are scheduled by The Nature Conservancy, which now owns this and many other such island preserves throughout the state. The excursion boat ***Argo*** offers a two-hour cruise around Damariscove Island. The cruise is narrated by Captain Peter Ripley, who gives an entertaining and informative talk while carefully maneuvering his boat among the ledges and outcrops where seals and other waterfowl can be observed.

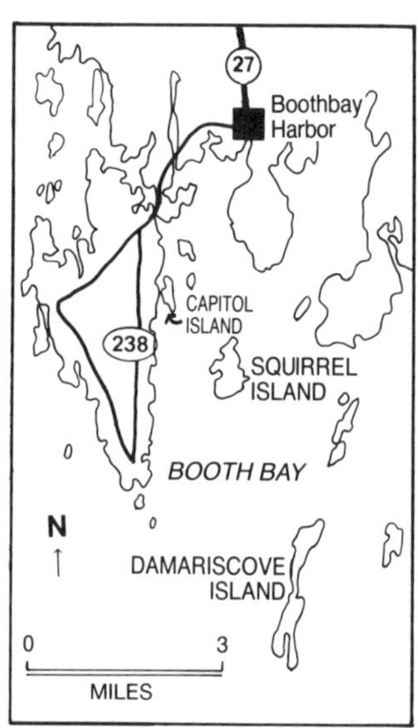

Boothbay Harbor Islands

About three miles out to sea from Boothbay Harbor lies **Squirrel Island,** Maine's oldest summer colony. The early history of the island is vague, but for the one hundred or so families that summer here now, the story began with their ancestors.

In the late 1800s it was not unusual for a number of families to form an association and purchase an island for their private summer use. The association generally would own the land, while families would own their individual cottages. The cottages almost never passed out of the hands of the original families; hence, today, fourth and fifth generations enjoy a lifestyle reminiscent of bygone days. Squirrel Island has been owned by just such an association since 1870.

About one hundred homes occupy this island, which is a mile long and barely a half-mile wide. While they have electricity, there are no private telephones, no cars, and not even any bikes. Everyone walks, and there is a veritable maze of paved sidewalks — five miles' worth — going off in every direction.

A small ferry, the ***Maranbo II,*** cruises out to the island during the summer, and while all property is private, no one seems to object to a casual visitor who sticks to the paths. The island's only shops are a **Tea Shop** (''for members only'') and two small gift shops. One gift shop, **Acorn Hollow,** specializes in Squirrel Island products — T-shirts, note paper, and cards. The other, the interesting **Indian Basket**

Store, sells handmade moccasins and baskets, one even called the Squirrel Island Basket. Sadie Ranco Mitchell, who runs the shop, is one of the few remaining descendants of the Penobscots, a tribe of Abnaki Indians who summered on Squirrel Island as long ago as the 1600s. The association set aside a piece of land for the Penobscots' exclusive use, on which the small shop and a house are built. The special basket made for the island is long and cylindrical with wheels so that islanders can transport their groceries and belongings from the ferry landing along the miles of sidewalks to their houses.

On Squirrel Island everyone transports his own goods home from the ferry landing along the miles of sidewalks.

The serenity and beauty of Squirrel Island had a particular attraction to some of the country's outstanding twentieth-century poets. At least three Pulitzer Prize winners summered here over the years: Theodore Roethke, Robert Penn Warren, and Anne Sexton. Sexton spent many childhood summers here and returned to the island for the centennial celebration in 1971 to give a reading of her poems.

A good time to visit the island is on a Sunday morning when you can attend a religious service in the beautiful century-old island **chapel.** *Maranbo II* makes special trips out to the island and back on Sunday mornings for those wishing to attend the nondenominational service.

Capitol Island, another "step back in time," is connected to Southport Island by a bridge so tiny that only one car can cross it at a time. Southport forms the eastern shore of Boothbay Harbor and has been connected to the mainland for years by a drawbridge. Capitol is strictly a summer colony — a gate closes off the bridge in winter — and there are about forty-five cottages on it. It was formerly called Pig Island but was renamed by the islanders, a group of friends, most of whom came here around the turn of the century from the area of Augusta, the "capital" of Maine.

The price of a room is an incredible holdover from the nineteenth century and even includes a fresh-baked wild blueberry muffin breakfast.

One of the more attractive things about Capitol Island is the **Albonegon Inn** (pronounced al-buh-NEE-gun). The only inn on the island, it describes itself as "determinedly old-fashioned," and that it is. Built in the late 1800s, it is a comfortable old inn, perched on the water's edge, where guests can sit and chat while rocking on the wide front veranda on a warm night, or sit and chat inside by a cozy fire on a cool night. The price of a room (with a sink but shared bath) is an incredible holdover from the nineteenth century and even includes a fresh-baked wild blueberry muffin breakfast.

The inn does not serve lunch or dinner, but just across the bridge in Southport is **Robinson's Wharf,** where you can enjoy lobsters and clams served at picnic tables. Here, too, the price is right.

ACCESS

BOOTHBAY HARBOR. Directions: From I-95 (Maine Turnpike) take exit 9 to Route 1 north. From Wiscasset, take Route 27 south to Boothbay Harbor and the waterfront area. There is a fee for the parking lot.

ARGO. **Directions:** Departs from Pier 6 (Fisherman's Wharf) in Boothbay Harbor. **Season:** Tuesday and Friday during July and August. **Admission:** Charged. **Telephone:** (207) 633-4925 or 633-5090.

MARANBO II. **Directions:** Departs from Pier 8 (Chimney Pier) in Boothbay Harbor. **Season:** Seven trips a day in the summer, reduced schedule off-season and winter. **Admission:** Charged. **Telephone:** (207) 633-2284.

DAMARISCOVE ISLAND PRESERVE. For information about field trips to this and other island preserves, write to The Nature Conservancy, 20 Federal Street, Brunswick, ME 04011, or call (207) 729-5181.

ACORN HOLLOW. Directions: From the ferry landing follow the sidewalk path to the left. Turn right at the post office and pass the chapel (on your left) and the outdoor pump. At the next intersection you will see a small sign in front of a large, rambling cottage on your left. **Season:** July and August.

INDIAN BASKET STORE. Directions: From the ferry landing follow the sidewalk path to the left past the post office. The basket shop is on your left (next to the tennis courts). **Season:** Intermittently during July and August.

SQUIRREL ISLAND CHAPEL. Directions: From the ferry landing follow the sidewalk path to the left. At the first intersection (by the post office) go right. The chapel will be a short distance along on your left. **Season:** July and August.

ALBONEGON INN. Directions: Continue south on Route 27 from Boothbay Harbor to Route 238 south. You will see a large sign on your left for Albonegon Inn. Follow the road indicated by this sign, cross the small bridge, and the inn is on your left at the water's edge. **Telephone:** (207) 633-2521.

ROBINSON'S WHARF. Directions: From Boothbay Harbor, follow Route 27 south to Southport. Just after crossing the drawbridge you will see Robinson's on your left. **Season:** Restaurant, mid-June to early September; fish market open year-round. **Telephone:** (207) 633-3830 or 633-3033.

PENOBSCOT BAY

If you've ever heard the expressions "the rock-bound coast of Maine" or "the country of the pointed firs," you have heard the two best descriptions of Maine's largest bay area, the Penobscot. Thirty-five miles long, the coastline here was deeply gouged during the Ice Age. Left in the glacier's wake were hundreds of peninsulas, inlets, islands, and outcrops, along with some of the most prized sailing waters along the New England coast.

The bay was first explored by the English explorer Martin Pring in 1603. A year later, the French explorer Samuel de Champlain claimed it for France. Many early trading posts and missions were established here, and for years the possession of the bay was highly disputed among the French, English, and Americans.

Shipbuilding, lumbering, and, of course, fishing became important industries, and by the mid-eighteenth century the beauty of the bay had been discovered by the summer rusticators. The bay has been called a Down East paradise for yachtsmen, and throughout the summer months it is plied by the famous windjammer fleet out of Camden and Rockport.

The library building on North Haven Island is a model of New England charm and simplicity.

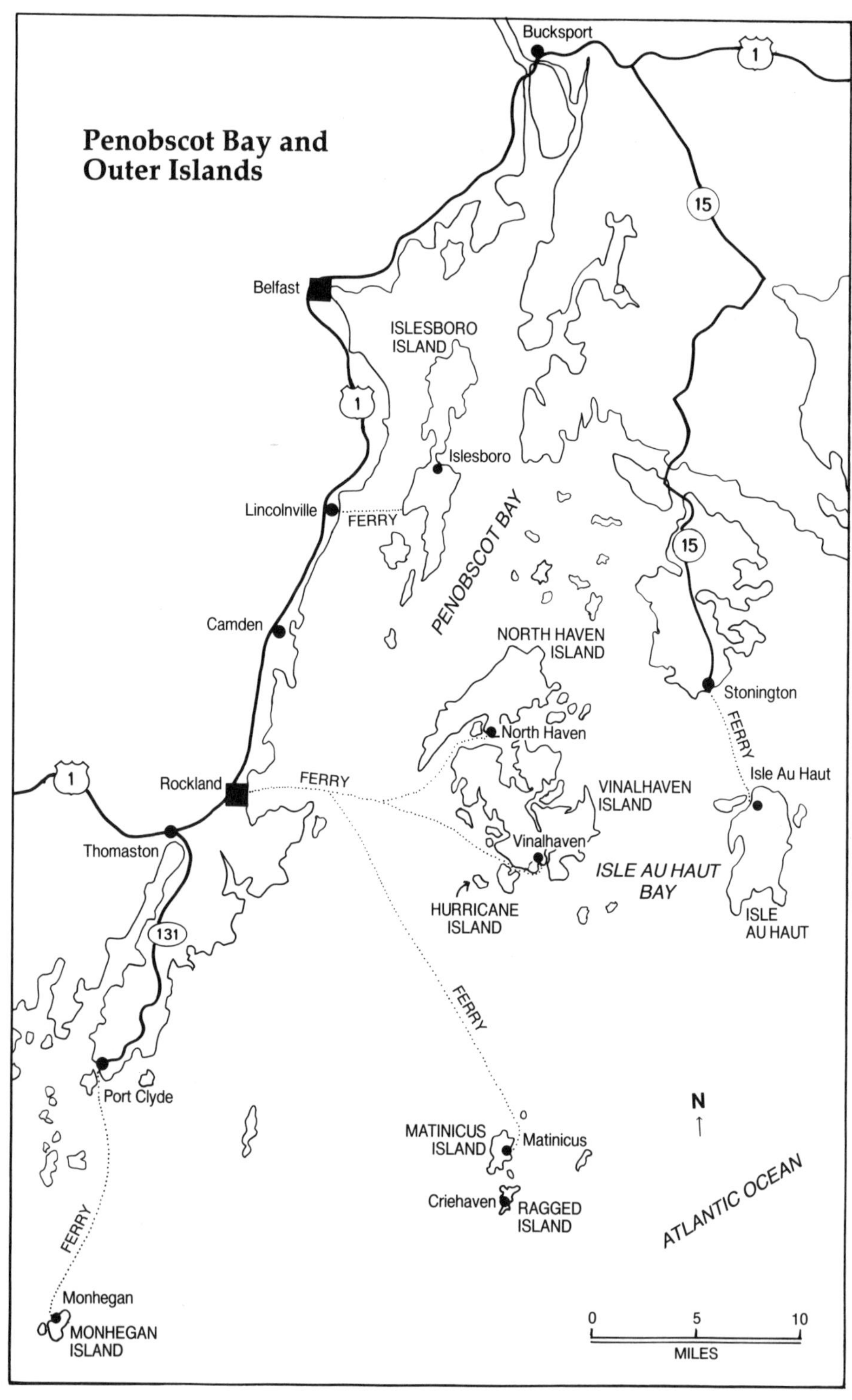

Penobscot Bay and Outer Islands
Bucksport
1
15
Belfast
ISLESBORO ISLAND
1
Islesboro
Lincolnville
FERRY
PENOBSCOT BAY
15
Camden
NORTH HAVEN ISLAND
Stonington
North Haven
FERRY
1
Rockland
FERRY
VINALHAVEN ISLAND
Isle Au Haut
Thomaston
Vinalhaven
ISLE AU HAUT BAY
HURRICANE ISLAND
ISLE AU HAUT
131
FERRY
Port Clyde
N
MATINICUS ISLAND
Matinicus
Criehaven
RAGGED ISLAND
ATLANTIC OCEAN
FERRY
Monhegan
MONHEGAN ISLAND
0
5
10
MILES

If you've always wanted a taste of "real" sailing in a tall ship, a windjammer cruise around the Penobscot is a great way to go. Sailing from a number of ports along the coast — particularly Camden and Rockport — the ships take six-day cruises, leaving on Monday and returning on Saturday. You'll enjoy an itinerary of hands-on sailing (or not, as you wish), trips ashore to the islands for a clambake or sightseeing, a steady stream of delicious meals, an evening of singing old sea chanties, and a comfortable bunk to bed down in. You can choose from any number of beautiful old vessels and some newer reproductions.

If you've always wanted a taste of "real" sailing in a tall ship, a windjammer cruise around the Penobscot is a great way to go.

Some of the largest year-round island communities in Maine can be found in Penobscot Bay. Most islanders not only encourage summer visitors but depend on them for part of their livelihood. Some very nice inns, guesthouses, restaurants, shops, and recreation facilities are available.

ACCESS

ROCKLAND, ROCKPORT, AND CAMDEN are all located on Route 1. Take exit 9 from I-95 (Maine Turnpike).

THE MAINE WINDJAMMER ASSOCIATION. For information about cruises, write to the association at Box 317P, Rockport, ME 04856, or call (207) 236-4867.

ROCKLAND AREA CHAMBER OF COMMERCE. Harbor Park, P.O. Box 508, Rockland, ME 04841; (207) 596-0376.

North Haven

The Fox Islands Thorofare, separating North Haven from the northern side of Vinalhaven, is so narrow that, from a distance, the two islands look like one. And while for many years they were considered one township under the name Fox Islands, they are decidedly different in character.

The village of North Haven fronts on the Thorofare, thus making it a gathering place for boats of all description. During the summer, the Thorofare is crowded with a mix of sleek new yachts, old windjammers, little sailboats, North Haven dinghies, lobster boats, and sardine carriers.

Sailing as a sport has a long and important heritage on the island, which has strongly influenced sailboat racing throughout the country. The North Haven dinghies, small wooden boats with bluff bows and gaff-rigged sails, originated here and today constitute the oldest one-design sailboat racing class in America.

North Haven dinghies, small wooden boats with bluff bows and gaff-rigged sails, originated here and today constitute the oldest one-design sailboat racing class in America.

Most yachtsmen proclaim **Pulpit Harbor** on the northern end of the island one of the most beautiful and sheltered harbors in Penobscot Bay. It has been visited by an impressive list of yachting enthusiasts, including several U.S. presidents.

North Haven differs from the more bustling, commercial Vinalhaven in its quiet, elegant simplicity. While some farming and fishing still is done here, the island's economy is pretty much sustained by its summer residents and visitors. About three hundred people live on the island year-round, but the population swells to well over two thousand in the summer. "I often wonder where they all find beds," says innkeeper Almon Ames.

Al owns and runs **The Ames House,** a charming Victorian guesthouse where, at the sound of a tinkling dinner bell, a sumptuous seven-course dinner is served each evening in the candlelit dining room. He is a delightful host who offers guests free access to his well-stocked refrigerator and, on a chilly October evening, invites them to gather and chat around a warm, century-old wood stove in the kitchen.

North Haven's irregular shape almost defies measurement, but the best guess seems to call it eight miles at its longest point and about three miles at its widest. It is indented with numerous coves and harbors and has a large freshwater pond at its center. Paved roads, stretching out to all parts of the island, meander past sweeping farms and estates whose houses are prominently positioned to face the ocean.

Many of these homes have been the summer residences of several generations of wealthy, old New England families such as the Cabots, Saltonstalls, and Lamonts. The old Dwight Morrow house on Crabtree Point, where Charles Lindbergh often landed his light plane on the front lawn, still stands proudly facing out to sea. Anne Morrow Lindbergh spent some of her happiest days here and speaks fondly about North Haven in several of her books, particularly *North to the Orient*.

The old Dwight Morrow house on Crabtree Point, where Charles Lindbergh often landed his light plane on the front lawn, still stands proudly facing out to sea.

The village of North Haven has a few shops, an art gallery, a library, three churches, a couple of fish markets, and a general store. There is only one place to have lunch, **The Landing,** which is a take-out window with outdoor picnic tables. The **Pulpit Harbor Inn**, a two-mile walk from the village, serves a light lunch and dinner, but you must make reservations for the latter.

Although there are only a few shops on the island, the quality of their merchandise is superior. **Calderwood-Hall**, a first-rate art gallery in the village, displays an unusual collection of arts and crafts from the very talented hands of local craftspeople. Model ships — some restored antiques and some new — paintings in various media, wood carvings, professional photographs, and sculpture, as well as fine hand-knitted and quilted items, woven cloth, and clothing are for sale.

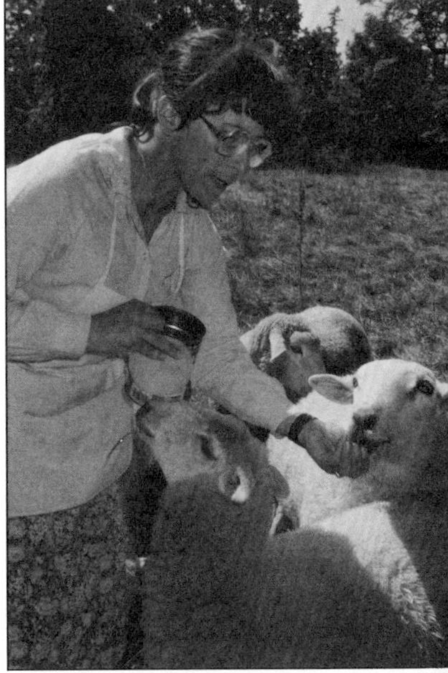

Weaver Jane Parsons gets the raw material for her creations from her own small flock of sheep.

This collection of crafts has only recently been put together by Jane and Herb Parsons. "We had no idea of just what we would get when we started this project," Jane says, "but the quality of crafts is just what we had hoped for." Jane often sits at her spinning wheel or loom while on duty at the gallery, spinning the wool from her own sheep that are bleating away just down the street. Surrounded by baskets of freshly dyed wool, Jane points to each affectionately, saying, "This is Emily, and this is McDuff, and the lavender casserole (because the wool was dyed lavender in a casserole bowl) is from Minerva — who not only gave me nine and a half pounds of wool but triplets — two black and one white."

Like many of Maine's more remote island communities once supported by merchant vessels, fishing, and the granite industry, North Haven has seen a rapid decline in its population during this century (twenty percent in this past decade alone). Young people, no longer able to find jobs and to maintain the family homestead, are forced to leave, selling houses to summer vacationers who are willing to pay high prices, which, in turn, inflate property values on the island. In recent years, islanders have joined together to seek new ways to increase economic opportunities on North Haven. Calderwood-Hall is one such effort, and **North Island Yarn** is another. Operating from a large shop in the village, owner Chellie Pingree, with the help of Jean White and Debby Anderson, employs more than twenty island women who make hand-knitted items and clothing for the shop. The women work at home, and the shop provides the supplies (yarn from island sheep) and the market.

The shop is open all summer and fall and one day a week in the winter. It is located next to the town's automatic laundry, and, says Jean White, "Women come in while their laundry is washing

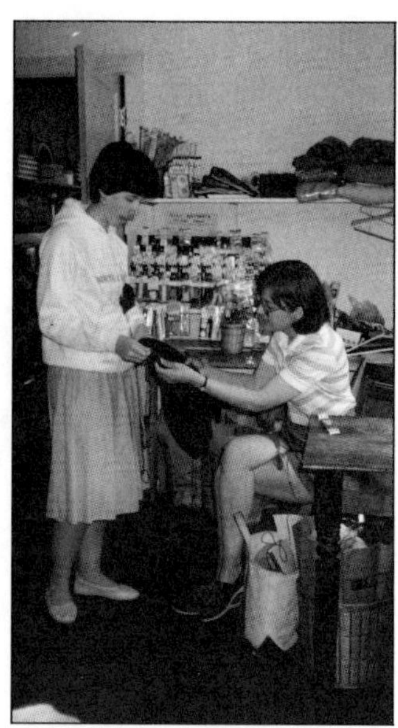

North Island Yarn's Jean White checks a work-in-progress.

and bring their knitting. With the wood stove going and the coffeepot on, it's very cozy."

Jean, whose husband is superintendent of schools ("I think they hired him because we have five kids," she says, laughing, "which increased the school enrollment by seven percent!"), has some positive things to say about raising kids on an island. "I can't think of a better place for kids to grow up. They learn to take responsibility and become meaningful members of the community early. There are only so many people to fill all the slots that need to be filled."

North Island Yarn also has a mail-order business, making custom-knitted sweaters and selling custom-designed knitting kits. Jean White designs many of the kits, and Doreen Cabot makes many of the classic skirts and blouses.

Both the Pulpit Harbor Inn and The Ames House are open year-round, and both places provide bicycles for guests. There is a **taxi service** on the island as well. Fall is one of the prettiest times to visit the island. There are deer- and duck-hunting seasons and places for ice skating and cross-country skiing in the winter.

ACCESS

ROCKLAND. Directions: Take exit 9 from I-95 (Maine Turnpike). Follow Route 1 to Main Street and follow the "Ferry" signs to the dock.

MAINE STATE FERRY SERVICE. Directions: The *North Haven* to the island leaves from and returns to the terminal on Main Street several times a day. The trip takes 1 hour and 10 minutes each way. The ferry carries both cars and passengers, and there is a parking lot (fee) at the dock. **Season:** Year-round. **Admission:** Charged. **Telephone:** (207) 863-4421.

STONINGTON FLYING SERVICE. Takes passengers on the daily mail plane and offers charter flights. **Directions:** From Rockland (Route 1) turn right onto South Main Street (Route 73) and continue out toward Owls Head. Take a left turn onto Ash Point Road, following signs to Knox County Airport and Stonington Flying Service. **Season:** Year-round. **Admission:** Charged. **Telephone:** (207) 596-6211.

THE AMES HOUSE. Directions: From the ferry landing, follow the main road to the left. Take the next left (Dole Road) to Browns Cove. The Ames House is at the end of the road (follow the signs). (The inn is about a 20-minute walk from the village to Browns Cove. Taxi service is available.) **Season:** Year-round. **Telephone:** (207) 867-4853.

THE LANDING. Directions: A short walk up from the ferry landing on the main road. **Season:** Memorial Day to Labor Day. **Telephone:** (207) 867-2060.

PULPIT HARBOR INN. Directions: From the ferry landing follow the main road, taking a left at the first intersection. Continue on this road to the next intersection, and the inn is on your left (2-mile walk from the village). (If you have reservations at the inn, transportation will be provided to and from the ferry landing.) **Season:** Year-round. **Telephone:** (207) 867-2219.

CALDERWOOD-HALL. Directions: Walk up from the ferry, turning right onto the main road. Calderwood-Hall is on the left. **Season:** Memorial Day to Labor Day. **Admission:** Free.

NORTH ISLAND YARN. Directions: Walk up from the ferry, turning right onto the main road. The shop is a short distance down on your right. **Season:** Year-round (one day a week in winter). **Admission:** Free. **Telephone:** (207) 867-2004.

TINY TAXI. Telephone: (207) 867-2076.

J. O. BROWN & SON BOATYARD. Water taxi to Vinalhaven. **Telephone:** (207) 867-4621.

Vinalhaven

Ever hear of a galamander? Any child on Vinalhaven can tell you what one is. An original galamander stands right in the middle of the small village green on Vinalhaven, and it's painted "Littlefield blue," after Rev. W.H. Littlefield, once pastor of the local Union Church, who invented the vehicle and painted it this color. The galamander, a wagon made of sturdy oak with enormous nine-foot wheels, hauled huge slabs of granite from the quarries down to the water's edge to the waiting "stone sloops." (For more on stone sloops, see Casco Bay — Great and Little Chebeague.) To the villagers, it's a symbol of the community's turn-of-the-century heritage as one of the leading granite-quarrying areas in the country.

Ever hear of a galamander? Any child on Vinalhaven can tell you what one is.

Vinalhaven granite, pink and blue-gray, specked with black and white, resembles marble when polished to a high shine. It was prized by leading architects and sculptors, who used it in monuments such as Grant's Tomb, Cathedral of St. John the Divine, the United States Post Office in Washington, D.C., and the New York Custom House. At the height of the island's quarry days in

Young fishermen await a bite at the dock in Vinalhaven.

the late nineteenth century, more than fifteen hundred men were employed in the quarrying and carving of stone.

The appearance of concrete and other artificial building and paving materials on the market in the early 1900s signaled the end of the quarrying industry. When that happened, islanders turned back to the old tradition of fishing, and today that is still the main industry here. More than two hundred lobster boats set out each day from Vinalhaven all year long, and in the late summer and early fall, seining is still practiced in the island's many coves.

At the height of the island's quarry days in the late nineteenth century, more than fifteen hundred men were employed in the quarrying and carving of stone.

The **quarries,** although abandoned by the stonecutters, provide swimmers with some of the most beautiful man-made pools you can imagine. On any sunny day in summer, these huge pools, fed with clear spring water, resonate with the sounds of shouting, splashing swimmers. Not only do the quarries make excellent swimming holes, but in some, trout and other freshwater fish thrive, providing the angler with an opportunity for a change from deep-sea fishing.

Vinalhaven is the largest and most populated island (twelve hundred year-round residents) in the bay. It is about nine and a half miles long and four and a half miles wide. The village nestles around Carver's Cove. A paved road winds up from the ferry dock, past a small motel, some elderly housing apartments, several shops, a few restaurants, and a post office. Most of the houses on the island are clustered around the village, having been built long before there were cars on the island.

Although you can take your car to the island, the roads lend themselves more to bicycling. At any one of the local stores you can buy a **Bicycle Route and Street Map,** which charts a two-and-a-half-hour bike route, indicating paved and dirt roads as well as many scenic spots on the island. The shape of Vinalhaven is such that you are almost never more than a mile from the ocean.

The shape of Vinalhaven is such that you are almost never more than a mile from the ocean.

Several people also offer **taxi service** and give tours. Bob Noonan is one of them. Bob does only a few tours now, as he keeps pretty busy with runs back and forth to the small island airport, transporting the mail and picking up passengers. But you couldn't have a more thorough introduction to the island than Bob provides. His sense of humor peppers his running commentary on island history. "People always ask me what we do on this island," he says, deadpan, "and I tell them, all summer long we fish and make love — and during the winter — we don't fish."

Bob's tour includes a trip up **Tip Toe Mountain** to reveal the panoramic view of the island overlooking Crockett's Cove and Dogfish Island. At the right time of year you may see small boats bobbing in the water below, piled high with seining nets, ready and waiting for the shoals of herring to appear. If time allows, you may also get to drive over to **Brown's Head Light** to catch the sunset. A manned Coast Guard lighthouse perched at the water's edge, it overlooks the Fox Islands Thorofare, North Haven Island, and the Camden Hills beyond. It is a beautiful sight.

There are several parks and nature preserves around the island, some within easy walking distance of the village. You'll also find a children's playground, trails for hiking, and several sandy beaches for sunning and swimming. **Lane's Island Preserve**, connected to Vinalhaven by a small causeway over Indian Creek, is a forty-five-acre recreational preserve with beaches and trails leading to the rocky outer shore where, on windy days, the surf is quite spectacular.

Long used for recreation by islanders, Lane's was threatened in 1968 by commercial development. Determined residents of Vinalhaven, with the help of The Nature Conservancy, worked hard and quickly to raise the funds necessary to purchase the land and to insure that it would be kept open to the public forever.

The **Annual Fourth of July Town Picnic** is held here and is just a ten-minute walk from the village. Visitors are encouraged to check in at the registration box and to pass along any observations or comments. Visitors have come from as far away as New Zealand, France, and Sweden.

Several places on the island accommodate overnight guests. **The Tidewater Motel** and the **Fox Island Inn** are highly recommended. The Tidewater Motel, just up the road from the ferry landing, is right on the water, and most units have small balconies overlooking the harbor. The units are clean and comfortable, and the owners, Mr. and Mrs. Arthur Crossman, are very accommodating.

On the other side of the village is the Fox Island Inn. It's an old Victorian, spacious and newly redecorated by owners Peter Sandefur and Anita Kellogg. According to Anita, the inn used to be the home of a midwife, and many island babies were born here. The former "birthing" room is now a cozy sitting room. Piping hot coffee, juice, and muffins are ready for the earliest risers in the morning.

Along with a few stores where you can purchase food and snack items, the village has several restaurants. **Sands Cove Lobster & Clambake** is close to the dock and serves freshly caught seafood "in the rough." **The Harbor Gawker** is popular well into the night, and there's always a crowd around the take-out window, where you can buy everything from a live lobster (they'll cook it for you) to a cone of soft ice cream with jimmies.

Throughout the summer there are **band concerts** at the brightly painted town bandstand and a series of **classical music concerts** in the Union Church. An **Arts and Crafts Show and Sale** usually is held each August, and events sponsored by the local historical society add much in the way of entertainment.

If you want to take a trip to nearby North Haven Island, you can easily arrange it by contacting the **water taxi** service. It takes only a few minutes to cross the Fox Island Thorofare. The fee is nominal.

ACCESS

ROCKLAND. Directions: Take exit 9 from I-95 (Maine Turnpike). Follow Route 1 to Main Street and follow the "Ferry" signs to the dock.

MAINE STATE FERRY SERVICE. Directions: The *Gov-*

ernor Curtis to Vinalhaven leaves from and returns to the terminal on Main Street several times a day. The trip takes 1 hour and 25 minutes. The ferry carries both cars and passengers, and there is a parking lot (fee) at the dock. **Season:** Year-round. **Admission:** Charged. **Telephone:** (207) 594-5543.

STONINGTON FLYING SERVICE. Takes passengers on the daily mail plane and offers charter flights. **Directions:** From Rockland (Route 1) turn right onto South Main Street (Route 73) and continue out toward Owls Head. Take a left turn onto Ash Point Road, following signs to Knox County Airport and Stonington Flying Service. **Season:** Year-round. **Admission:** Charged. **Telephone:** (207) 596-6211.

Long abandoned by stonecutters, Vinalhaven's quarries now make ideal swimming places.

BOOTH QUARRY. Directions: (About 2½ miles from village.) From ferry landing turn right onto Main Street, which becomes Pequot Road. Quarry is close to the road on your right and has a parking lot. **Season:** Year-round. **Admission:** Free.

LAWSON QUARRY. Directions: (About 1 mile from ferry.) From the ferry turn left onto Main Street and then right onto North Haven road. Quarry is on your right (close to the road). **Season:** Year-round. **Admission:** Free.

BOB NOONAN'S TAXI SERVICE. (207) 863-4378.

LANE'S ISLAND PRESERVE. Directions: (About 1 mile from ferry.) From the ferry landing turn right onto Main Street. Follow Main Street past the last business block and turn right onto Water Street, which runs into Atlantic Avenue. Cross the Lane's Island Bridge to the preserve. (Brochures are available free at most stores and inns.) **Season:** Year-round. **Admission:** Free.

THE TIDEWATER MOTEL. Directions: From the ferry landing walk straight up the road toward the village. The motel is on your right. **Season:** Year-round. **Telephone:** (207) 863-4618.

FOX ISLAND INN. Directions: From the ferry landing walk up to the village. Turn left onto Main Street. Walk past the library, turning left onto Carver Street. The inn is the fifth building on the left. **Season:** Year-round. **Telephone:** (207) 863-2122.

SANDS COVE LOBSTER & CLAMBAKE. Directions: This outdoor restaurant is located to the left of the ferry landing on Sands Road (a short walk). **Season:** Memorial Day to Labor Day (closed on Tuesdays). **Telephone:** (207) 863-2171 or 863-2559.

THE HARBOR GAWKER. Directions: From the ferry landing walk straight up West Main Street. The Gawker is on your left. **Season:** May through September. **Telephone:** (207) 863-9365.

WATER TAXI TO NORTH HAVEN. (207) 867-4621.

Hurricane Island

As the ferry threads its way through the Laireys Narrows, toward the southern side of Vinalhaven, you pass a number of small islands, one of which is Hurricane. Like Vinalhaven, Hurricane prospered during the "granite days." A quarry was started here in 1870, and a sizable town sprang up. At one point about fifteen hundred people worked on the island, and many families lived in the sixty-five houses and several boarding houses here. Skilled stonecutters and artisans came from as far away as Italy and Sweden to work in the quarries. With the demise of the industry the population quickly dispersed, and for many years the island was deserted.

Since 1941, however, Hurricane Island has been the location of an **Outward Bound** school. The concept of Outward Bound began during the Second World War when it was noted that young British sailors, although physically fit, were less able to survive sea disasters than older, more experienced, though less physically fit men. The idea of exposing students to a series of supervised but challenging survival tests in a wilderness situation has proved tremendously successful and educational.

The Hurricane Island Outward Bound Sea School is the only one of its kind in the Western Hemisphere.

The Hurricane Island Outward Bound Sea School, which provides students with the opportunity to understand, test, and demonstrate their own resources in a wilderness environment, is the only one of its kind in the Western Hemisphere. It offers courses ranging from six to twenty-six days that are open to men and women ages sixteen and a half to sixty. The year-round program includes courses in sailing, sea kayaking, canoeing, cycling, backpacking, winter camping, technical rock climbing, cross-country skiing, and snowshoeing.

During the summer school season (May to October) visitors in private boats are welcome to the island, and, when available, a member of the program will conduct a tour at your request. During the winter months courses are held in the mountains of western Maine and New Hampshire.

ACCESS

HURRICANE ISLAND OUTWARD BOUND SEA SCHOOL. P.O. Box 429, Rockland, ME 04841; (800) 341-1744 (toll-free); in Maine, (207) 594-5548.

Sailor's Memorial Museum on Islesboro includes the now inactive Grindle Point lighthouse.

Islesboro

Poets and songwriters around the world have immortalized locations renowned for their glorious sunsets. For many New Englanders, however, nothing could surpass the sight of the sun going down behind the Camden Hills of Maine, reflecting off the shimmering waters of Penobscot Bay. And one of the choice observation points from which to witness this glorious spectacle, as attested by the number of stately mansions built along its western banks, is an elegant little island called Islesboro.

New Englanders are not alone in their devotion to this area. Presidents, royalty, and millionaires, including the Astors, Rothschilds, Biddles, Anthony Edens, and Marshall Fields, have come from far and wide to enjoy the sight. Many of their heirs still summer in the town of Dark Harbor on the southern tip of the island, said to be one of the wealthiest summer colonies in the country.

It is fitting, of course, that the **Islesboro Inn** is located in Dark Harbor. This large, white, gabled building, surrounded by well-groomed lawns and colorful flower beds, was built in the early 1900s as a private "cottage" with all its bedrooms facing the sea. It's the type of place, rare on any Maine island, where you can choose to have breakfast in your canopied bed or in front of your own private fireplace. Sailing, tennis, and bicycling (the inn will prepare a picnic lunch for you) are the main events on Islesboro. Except, that is, for the sunset, which is *the* highlight of the day. Long before sunset, guests begin to gather on the gently sloping lawn or wide stone patio of the inn in anticipation of the event.

Sailors also partake of the inn's elegance. A

bright yellow canopy jutting out over the terrace acts as a beacon to tall-masted schooners — windjammers — that head into the harbor for the night. After watching the sunset and dining aboard ship, passengers from the windjammers are motored in by their captains or crew members for a nightcap in the lounge.

Inn guests dine in quiet elegance by candlelight, with fresh flowers and crisp linens adorning the table. After dinner you may play cards in the game room or join the conversation and socializing before a crackling fire in the front room's large marble fireplace. Or you might want to join the "windjammers" in the lounge, who probably will have begun to sing old sea chanties or swap fish stories.

Inn guests dine in quiet elegance by candlelight with fresh flowers and crisp linen adorning the table.

Actually, the name of this island is not Islesboro but Long Island. Long Island, being such a common name in these parts, soon gave way to Islesboro, the name of the largest of the three towns on the island. The township to which Islesboro belongs also includes a number of small islands, most notably **Seven Hundred Acre Island,** where Charles Dana Gibson built a rambling mansion, and remote **Warren Island,** where, if you have your own boat, you can camp and picnic.

In 1779, just off the shores on the northern tip of Islesboro, occurred the largest naval engagement of the American Revolution — and one of the most disastrous for the colonists. More than a thousand men under General Solomon Lovell, Commander Dudley Saltonstall, and Lieutenant Colonel Paul Revere were sent to drive the British out of Castine (a small town on the mainland opposite Islesboro). While the leaders set to bickering among themselves, a fleet of British frigates appeared, forcing the Americans to retreat. Every American ship was lost, and the men who managed to escape had to walk all the way back to Boston. Revere was court-martialed on charges of cowardice and disobedience for his part in the battle, but he was later cleared. An ancient house in Pripet (on the northeastern side of the island) still has a hole in it from a British cannonball fired during this famous battle.

Islesboro lies in the middle of Penobscot Bay, but it is only three miles off the mainland at Lincolnville Beach. It's just a twenty-minute ride on the Maine State Ferry, ***Governor Muskie***, which carries cars as well as people. The ferry runs almost hourly during the summer (less frequently in other seasons), so Islesboro is one of the more accessible Maine islands. Also, because the ferry docks at the remote Grindle Point, a few miles from the main road, it's best to have your car or a bike to get around.

The island, which is ten miles long, is quite spread out, with no central village to speak of. The main road along which the island's few stores and shops are located runs the length of the island and is very narrow at points, affording great views of scenic harbors and small coves for exploring. **Dark Harbor** is a popular stopping place for bikers. It has a nice restaurant **(The Blue Heron),** a grocery store, a real estate office, and the **Dark Harbor Shop**, which offers deli sandwiches, ice cream, maps, and souvenirs. **Dark Harbor House,** a gracious bed and breakfast in a former summer "cottage" belonging to one of the Astors, is located close by. Sidney Sheldon, in his best-selling novel *Master of the Game,* featured Dark Harbor, calling it "the jealously guarded colony of the super-rich."

There are several public beaches, picnic areas, and walking trails, particularly around the northern tip of the island, called **Turtle Head,** where you might catch a glimpse of a great blue heron. The island is fairly flat with more than twenty miles of paved road, so it's ideal for biking. No bike rentals are available on the island, but the inn has a few bikes for guests to use. A nine-hole golf course is open to the public for a fee.

Beautiful old homes such as this are in generous supply on Islesboro.

The old lighthouse at Grindle Point, no longer in use, is now part of the **Sailor's Memorial Museum** which is an interesting place to visit. You can investigate the old lighthouse, view exhibits of the island's maritime history, and examine artifacts of island life. The **Alice L. Pendleton Memorial Library** and the **Islesboro Historical Society** (in the former town hall) offer lots of fascinating reading and photographs relating to the "old days" on the island. The historical society sponsors a series of events throughout the summer to showcase the talents of local artisans.

Among the island's several antique shops are **The Swallow's Nest** ("real beautiful things . . . old and new," according to Lydia, the proprietor) and **Beaver Dam Antiques**. The latter is located in a former square-dance hall, and while the hall is no longer in use, square-dancing remains a popular activity on the island, with dances and callers arranged by the historical society several times during the year. (Look for notices of these and other events posted on a bulletin board at **Leach's Market** near the post office.)

The island boasts several bed and breakfast establishments, and while there are no campgrounds, some home owners rent rooms or allow camping, by permit, on their land. For more information and a free map of the island contact the Islesboro town manager.

Stonington Flying Service out of Owls Head (three miles from Rockland) provides charter flights to Islesboro. There is no taxi service on the island. If you are staying at one of the inns, you must make prior arrangements to be picked up. It's about two miles to the closest store. Islesboro has few street names. One main road runs the length of the island and loops back, and there are only a few side roads. Locations are known by names such as Turtle Head (northernmost point), Pendleton Point (southernmost point), and Dark Harbor. It's a good idea to obtain a map prior to arriving on the island.

ACCESS

MAINE STATE FERRY, LINCOLNVILLE. Directions: Follow Route 1 north through Camden. Lincolnville is about four miles north of Camden, and the ferry terminal (well-marked) is on your right. Parking is available. **Season:** Year-round. **Admission:** Charged. **Telephone:** (207) 789-5611.

STONINGTON FLYING SERVICE. Directions: From I-95, take exit 9 to Route 1 and Rockland. From the center of Rockland, take South Main Street (Route 73) south to Owls Head and follow signs to Knox County Airport. Turn left onto Ash Point Road where the Stonington Flying Service hangar is located. **Telephone:** (207) 596-6211.

ISLESBORO INN. Directions: After getting off the ferry, follow Ferry Road and take the first three right turns. **Season:** June 1 through October 31. **Telephone:** (207) 734-2222.

DARK HARBOR HOUSE. Directions: Follow Ferry Road out to the main road. Go south, following signs to Dark Harbor, past the Dark Harbor Shop. The house will be on your right. **Season:** June through September. **Telephone:** (207) 734-6669.

SAILOR'S MEMORIAL MUSEUM. Directions: Located in the old lighthouse at the ferry landing. **Season:** Mid-June through Labor Day. **Admission:** Free.

HISTORICAL SOCIETY. Directions: From the ferry landing follow Ferry Road to West Road (first intersection). Turn left onto West Road and follow it to the end. The historical society is on your left. **Season:** Mid-June through August. **Admission:** Free.

ALICE L. PENDLETON MEMORIAL LIBRARY. Directions: From the ferry landing follow Ferry Road to West Road (first intersection). Turn left onto West Road and follow it to the end where it intersects Main Road. Turn right onto Main Road and the library is on the next corner, at Hewes Point Road. **Season:** Year-round, Wednesdays, Saturdays, and Sundays only. **Admission:** Free.

THE SWALLOW'S NEST. Directions: From the ferry landing follow Ferry Road to West Road (first intersection). Turn left onto West Road and follow it to the end where it intersects with Main Road. Turn left onto Main Road and the shop is about 3 miles along on your left. **Season:** Mid-June through Labor Day.

BEAVER DAM ANTIQUES. Directions: From the ferry landing follow Ferry Road to West Road (first intersection). Turn left onto West Road and follow it to the end, where it intersects Main Road. Turn left onto Main Road and follow it to the intersection of Meadow Road, where the shop is located. **Season:** Mid-June through Labor Day. **Telephone:** (207) 734-6720.

ISLESBORO TOWN MANAGER. Town Office, Islesboro, ME 04848; (207) 734-6445.

OUTER ISLANDS

Far outside the craggy inland bays, in what is called the Gulf of Maine, lie several isolated island communities. Clinging tenaciously to a way of life that has endured for centuries, fisherfolk out here go about their business year-round tending their traps and seining nets and tolerating, to a certain degree, the ubiquitous summer visitor.

These islands are not for the novice island-hopper but more for those rugged individualists who share an affinity with the early coastal explorers. Civilization has been slow to invade these quiet places, where electricity and telephones are in short supply and transportation and communication still mean walking and talking.

Civilization has been slow to invade these quiet places, where electricity and telephones are in short supply and transportation and communication still mean walking and talking.

Nowhere on a Maine island can the water be colder, the fog thicker, the foghorns more mournful, the wind gustier, or the rains damper. But when it's a bright day, nowhere do the waters sparkle more clearly, the wildflowers smell more intoxicating, or the sun set more brilliantly. As a young Matinicus girl put it, "It's a wonderful place to live, but I wouldn't want to visit here." And it's true that you have to stick around a while to enjoy these islands fully.

Isle au Haut

Says the summer man, when the fog hangs low
There's a bridal wreath over Isle au Haut
But the fisherman says, when he launches his boat
It's gosh darn foggy off the Isle au Haut.

Chances are you'll pronounce the name wrong (no one seems to agree on whether it's "eel-oh-ho" or "aisle-a-holt" or "isle-a-ho").

Just mention the name "Isle au Haut" to someone from Maine and he or she is likely to recite this whimsical piece of doggerel to you. Chances are you'll pronounce the name wrong (no one seems to agree on whether it's "eel-oh-ho" or "aisle-a-holt" or "isle-a-ho"), but never mind, you'll be talking about one of the most breathtakingly beautiful islands off the coast of New England.

French navigator Samuel de Champlain gave it its name, meaning "high island," when he first spotted it on his cruise through Penobscot Bay in 1604. The heavily wooded and extraordinarily high hills rise at some points to more than five hundred fifty feet above sea level. These impressive peaks, visible for miles around and marking the eastern entrance to the bay, have served since Champlain's day as an important landmark to sailors.

To get to Isle au Haut, you must first traverse the Deer Islands, connected to the mainland by a bridge. Another series of bridges and causeways leads you to the Deer Islands' southernmost tip, the town of Stonington. The mail boat, *Miss Lizzy,* named for the much-loved ninety-four-year-old former postmistress, leaves Stonington for Isle au Haut at least twice a day year-round.

Winding in and out among a group of smaller islands, many of them former quarry sites but now deserted, the boat makes the eight-mile trip in about forty minutes. Off the northwestern side of Isle au Haut lies tiny Kimball Island, which borders the Isle au Haut Thorofare. Also nearby is Merchants Island with its single lonely and forlorn-looking large white house.

The relative inaccessibility and remoteness of Isle au Haut has protected it from an onslaught of tourists and made it a naturalist's dream. You'll find no hotels or guesthouses here, some electricity but no telephones, and only a campground for overnight accommodations (reservations required).

BARBARA SOUTHWORTH

The remoteness of Isle au Haut has helped to preserve that island's rugged beauty.

More than half the island was donated to **Acadia National Park** by heirs of some of the original owners. As all the island's public land is owned and operated by the park, a ranger is always on hand to meet visitors at the ferry landing (Town Dock). During the summer months an additional boat, the *Mink*, stops at **Duck Harbor** to deposit campers and hikers within a quarter mile of the campgrounds. The rest of the year campers have to be prepared to backpack about five miles from Town Dock to the campsite.

There are five fairly large lean-to shelters at **Duck Harbor Campground,** each with room enough for five or six people. Plenty of deadwood can be found in the surrounding forest for the fireplaces. A pump supplies drinking water, and chemical and compost toilets are close by. This is a very popular campground, and reservations, limited to three days in-season (mid-June to mid-September) and five days in the spring and fall, fill up quickly.

The island, six miles long and three miles wide, is almost completely forested, and more than thirty miles of marked trails offer hikers the opportunity to explore wooded uplands, marshes, bogs, the rocky shoreline, and a mile-long freshwater lake. You can obtain a map of the trails from the park ranger, who will answer any questions you have and make suggestions regarding the conditions of the trails on any given day. During the summer months the rangers also provide guided hiking tours of the island.

The small village area of Isle au Haut is sparsely settled and has a combination post office/general store, a rustic town hall, an exceptionally pretty schoolhouse, and a century-old steepled church perched on a prominent hillside. A twelve-mile road loops the island, and although not all of it is paved, it is reasonably good for biking.

Visitors to Isle au Haut travel aboard the mailboat Miss Lizzie, *named for the island's beloved former postmistress.*

The houses and farms along the main road leading out of the village are widely separated, and from the road there is little sign of activity. Tall wire fences protect the numerous vegetable gardens from the many friendly but hungry deer that roam the island. An overall feeling of quiet and solitude reigns here.

During the late 1700s the abundant mackerel fishing grounds in surrounding waters supported a flourishing village community. But it was a hard and lonely life, and with the invention of the powerboat, providing quick access to the mainland, families left the island in record numbers. Soon only a handful of hardy fishermen and farmers remained.

In 1879 a wealthy Boston financier "rediscovered" Isle au Haut, finding the quiet seclusion that had driven the former occupants away to be exactly what he and his bachelor friends were looking for. They bought most of the available land, formed a company, and built themselves a fine clubhouse. The **Point Lookout Club** opened in 1881 with a very exclusive membership. The first rule was that there were to be no women, children, or dogs allowed!

Eventually, however, the bachelors married, and large, comfortable family dwellings were built on the island. Now about three hundred people, mostly descendants of the original club members, make up the summer population. Most of the sixty-five or so year-round residents make their living by lobstering.

Another factor that keeps the island's population at a minimum in summer is the limit placed on the number of visitors each day. Acadia National

Park Authority, always mindful of the island's fragile ecology, never allows more than fifty visitors at one time. (This rarely causes a problem, but if you're planning a day trip in the middle of summer, you might want to call the park service before you go.) Whenever you visit, you'll no doubt see more deer and birds than people.

There are no public facilities in the village, and only one small general store operates on a limited schedule. If you are visiting for the day, or particularly if you are camping, it's wise to bring all your own food. The village of Stonington has a few small inns and restaurants as well as a store (close to the dock) where you can buy supplies before going to the island.

Acadia National Park Authority, always mindful of the island's fragile ecology, never allows more than fifty visitors at one time.

ACCESS

STONINGTON. Directions: From Route 1 in Bucksport continue northeast to Orland. Turn right onto Route 15. Follow Route 15 south to the end.

ISLE AU HAUT COMPANY. Directions: Both the *Mink* and the *Miss Lizzy* are docked at the Town Pier in Stonington, which is on your right as you enter the village. You may have to park your car in the school parking lot, a short walk from the dock (verify this when you telephone for schedules). **Season:** Year-round. **Admission:** Charged. **Telephone:** (207) 367-5193.

ACADIA NATIONAL PARK. For further information about Isle au Haut and camping reservations write to the park at P.O. Box 177, Bar Harbor, ME 04609, or call (207) 288-3338.

DEER ISLE–STONINGTON CHAMBER OF COMMERCE. Deer Isle, ME 04627; (207) 348-6124.

Monhegan Island

Artists have been flocking to Monhegan Island for decades. The renowned physical beauty of this place has attracted such art world luminaries as Edward Hopper, Rockwell Kent, Robert Henri, Jamie Wyeth, and John Hultberg, to name just a few. Many **artists,** at least a couple of dozen, live on the rugged little island year-round, and during the summer months most of their studios are open to visitors. You can obtain a flyer as soon as you get off the ferry showing the locations of each studio and giving the day and time each is open.

It's hard to believe that so much beauty is confined to such a tiny island. Only about one and a

The renowned physical beauty of this place has attracted such art world luminaries as Edward Hopper, Rockwell Kent, Robert Henri, Jamie Wyeth, and John Hultberg, to name just a few.

half miles in length and barely a mile wide, Monhegan rises up out of the ocean like a great gray whale, exposing cliffs more than one hundred feet high on one end. There's a rustic charm about Monhegan that sets it apart from other Maine islands. This is due, in part, to a concerted effort by the islanders, many of them writers, artists, and intellectuals, to keep modernization in check and to retain, as much as possible, the natural beauty of the island.

Monhegan rises up out of the ocean like a great gray whale, exposing cliffs more than one hundred feet high on one end.

Kerosene lamps and gaslights are used not for effect but out of necessity here. Electricity is home-generated, and, with the exception of the fully electrified Island Inn, most islanders rely on these dependable, old-fashioned devices every evening throughout the year. There are only a few telephones on the island; the one public phone is located next to the post office.

The village itself, a cluster of weathered cottages, inns, fishing shacks, and a few stores, lies on the sheltered southwestern slope of the island, facing a small harbor. A road of sorts leads toward the village from the town pier but quickly dissolves into a series of dirt paths that veer off in several directions. Except for a few emergency vehicles, there are no cars on the island and few bikes.

Monhegan (pronounced mon-E-g'n) is a hiker's paradise. More than seventeen miles of hiking trails suited to everyone from novice to expert crisscross a lush pine forest interlaced with sweet-smelling wildflowers and delicious berries. The trails extend out to quiet coves and pebbled beaches. You'll want to pick up a trail map as soon as you arrive (sold for ten cents or given free at guesthouses) to get your bearings.

Several trails lead out to the cliffs, affording a breathtaking panoramic view of the Atlantic. The cliffs can be very dangerous for walking or climbing, though. Slippery rocks and sudden large waves called combers are particularly threatening after a storm. Several accidents have occurred here — some of them fatal — so you should take precautions at all times.

Birding is another popular pastime on the island. In fact, you're apt to see more binoculars than sunglasses on any given day. This is particularly true during the spring and fall migration seasons, when visitors from various Audubon societies come to catch a glimpse of some rare species. But there is plenty to see all summer long (including a frolicsome population of seals that sun and play on the ledges just off the northern tip of the island). A

The traveler's options on Monhegan Island are many.

special boat trip with **Capt. Steve** out to Eastern Egg Rock provides an opportunity to view some rare Atlantic puffins.

Long before the white man arrived on Monhegan, Indians paddled their canoes out from the mainland each summer to fish and to enjoy the cooler climate. Several explorers are known to have stopped here. One, a Captain Edward Harlow, created some havoc when he took back to England two Indians whom he had abducted. It is known for sure that Captain John Smith arrived here in 1614 and claimed the island for England. A plaque commemorating this historic event is attached to a large boulder next to the schoolhouse.

More than seventeen miles of hiking trails suited to everyone from novice to expert crisscross a lush pine forest interlaced with sweet-smelling wildflowers and delicious berries.

Throughout most of the island's history, the chief industry has been fishing, and it remains so today. Monhegan lobstermen observe a very strict self-imposed code restricting their lobster season to January 1 through mid-June. Hence, all summer long huge piles of lobster traps and buoys line the harbor area. This restriction on lobstering during the summer insures the proper size and weight of future catches and has paid off well. Some lobster lovers, including those at *Boston* magazine, say the best lobsters in the world come from the shores of Monhegan.

While the island provides plenty of secluded nooks and crannies for quiet reading, sketching, or just plain daydreaming, there is always a pleasant flurry of activity around the village area. **Middle Beach**, popular with everyone for sunning and swimming and the safest beach for children, is located adjacent to the **Island Inn.** The wide front veranda of the inn is a favorite gathering place, and

Woodland fairies and trolls are rumored to dwell here, and island children (of all ages) see to it that tiny nature houses are made to accommodate them.

a friendly game of volleyball usually is going on in the backyard.

There are several little shops (the number fluctuates each season) in which to browse. Particularly interesting are local craft items — wood carvings, pottery, weaving, knitwear, photography, and paintings — for sale at **Winter Works. Plantation Gallery** exhibits local artists' work and offers many paintings for sale.

During the summer months a number of the many fishing boats bobbing in the harbor are available for deep-sea fishing trips, bird-watching expeditions, or sightseeing and exploring.

Monhegan has the reputation of being a quiet, somewhat Bohemian retreat for adults, but it is also a wonderful place for children. Not only is the island an exciting outdoor museum in and of itself, but there is also an indoor **museum,** located in the lighthouse and filled with instructive exhibits on local birds, flowers, and lobstering. There are trails and guided nature walks to enjoy (look for information about these on the large bulletin board near the general store), tidal pools and old shipwrecks to investigate, and tiny moss and twig houses in **Cathedral Woods** to inspect. Woodland fairies and trolls are rumored to dwell here, and island children (of all ages) see to it that tiny nature houses are made to accommodate them. Cathedral Woods derives its name from the effect created by the branches of tall spruces interlacing overhead and the green, moss-covered carpeting underfoot.

Monhegan lobstermen adhere to a strict code, working their traps from January 1 through mid-June only.

Little Manana Island, which lies in the harbor of Monhegan, acts as a barrier to the northwest winds and bears some interesting marks on a boulder at its summit. Some authorities have claimed that they are inscriptions put there by Norsemen or Phoenicians long before Europeans visited the island. You usually can find someone to row you to the island, where you can ascend a long wooden staircase to inspect the markings for yourself.

Monhegan is one of the most popular Maine islands for summer visitors and day-trippers, so if you plan to go there, you should make your reservations well in advance. The Island Inn, which is the only fully electrified lodging, offers the best accommodations but tends to cater to couples and singles. **The Trailing Yew**, with its simpler informal lodgings (shared bathrooms) and family-style meals, makes children feel right at home.

Ferry reservations from either Boothbay Harbor or Port Clyde, even for day-trippers, are at a premium during the peak summer months, so be sure to call at least a couple of days ahead.

As you are boarding the ferry to leave the island, you might be lucky enough to be handed a small bouquet of flowers. It's a very old custom for islanders to present their guests and friends with flowers grown in their own gardens (never wildflowers, which are not to be picked) as they leave the island — a token of island beauty to take home in remembrance of Monhegan.

The one-hour ferry trip to Monhegan allows just enough time to catch up on some reading.

ACCESS

PORT CLYDE. Directions: From I-95 (Maine Turnpike) take exit 9 to Route 1 and follow Route 1 to Thomaston. At Thomaston take Route 131 south to Port Clyde. Parking is available near the dock for ferry passengers.

MONHEGAN BOAT LINE. The *Laura B* makes two trips a day to Monhegan from mid-June through mid-September and one trip a day year-round. Steaming time is one hour, and advanced reservations are required. **Season:** Year-round. **Admission:** Charged. **Telephone:** (207) 372-8848.

BOOTHBAY HARBOR. Directions: Take I-95 (Maine Turnpike) to exit 9 and Route 1. Follow Route 1 to Wiscasset. From Wiscasset take Route 27 south to Boothbay Harbor and to the parking area on the wharf (fee).

***BALMY DAYS* (excursion boat).** Leaves once a day (early morning) from Boothbay Harbor, and passengers have four hours ashore on the island. Returns in the late afternoon. **Season:** June through September. **Admission:** Charged. **Telephone:** (207) 633-2284.

MONHEGAN ARTISTS. Directions: At the ferry landing is a box with flyers giving the locations of artists' studios and the prescribed times when you may visit them. Most of the studios are open in the afternoon only, from 2 to 5 P.M. **Season:** Mid-June to mid-September. **Admission:** Free.

CAPT. STEVE'S PUFFIN TOUR. Directions: Inquire at the Island Spa located at the top of the road from the ferry. **Season:** Mid-June to mid-September. **Admission:** Charged.

WINTER WORKS. Directions: A short walk up from the ferry landing, on the left at the top of the hill. **Season:** Mid-June to mid-September.

PLANTATION GALLERY. Directions: Take the road up from the ferry landing to the top of the hill. Just behind the Island Inn take the first right, toward the Perriwinkle Coffee Shop. The gallery is across the road on the left. **Season:** July and August.

MONHEGAN MUSEUM. Directions: Take the road from the ferry landing to the top of the hill. Continue past the Island Spa and follow signs to the lighthouse. **Season:** July and August. **Admission:** Free.

ISLAND INN. Directions: Take the road from the ferry landing to the top of the hill. The inn is on your right. **Season:** Mid-June through mid-September. **Telephone:** (207) 596-0371.

THE TRAILING YEW. Directions: Take the road up from the ferry. Turn right at the Island Spa and continue past the general store. Signs and path to the inn are on your right. **Season:** Mid-May to mid-October. **Telephone:** (207) 596-0440.

Matinicus and Criehaven

The Indians named it Matinicus, meaning "grassy island," but looking down on it from a small plane, it more resembles a dark green tuft of moss floating on the vast expanse of sea. A silver flash of rock, Matinicus Rock, catches your eye, and then two smaller tufts of dark green, Matinicus Island and Criehaven.

If you are serious about wanting to get away from it all, Matinicus or Criehaven may be just the place for you.

If you are serious about wanting to get away from it all, Matinicus or Criehaven may be just the place for you. You certainly won't have to worry about unexpected company dropping in, as these islands are not easy to get to. Matinicus, the larger of the two (all of two miles long and a mile wide), is the only one that has ferry service. But "that's only one day a month, and only if there's a boat available," says the woman at the transportation company. **Captain Albert Bunker,** who lives on Matinicus, runs a charter boat service to and from the island, but it's expensive.

Most islanders and visitors have come to rely on Herb and Charlie Jones, who operate the **Stonington Flying Service** out of Rockland. For fifteen dollars you can hop aboard their little Cessna that carries the mail out each morning around eight o'clock. They make a return flight around ten o'clock, or you can make special arrangements with them for a later flight back to the mainland.

Although the flight takes less than fifteen minutes, as you look down through the airplane windows at the small dots below, you get a sense of the islands' isolation from the mainland — twenty miles out to sea, with only some gulls and a few lobster boats circling the area. When making your

Matinicus is an island of bare essentials.

first flight to the island, it's easy to wonder just where on one of those tiny specks of earth you could possibly land. As you fly low over Matinicus, a corridor of parched grass miraculously appears amid the tall spruces, and before you have time to gasp, Charlie lands the plane along the narrow, bumpy strip with well-honed skill.

The village is just a short distance from the airport. It's an easy walk, but there's not much to see. The road is sparsely settled, although most of the seventy-five year-round residents live along this road rather than on the harbor, which often takes a beating in the winter. There's a large, handsome wooden church, a one-room schoolhouse surrounded by a playground, and a rather worrisome-looking fire engine that seems to represent the town fire department.

Another gravel road leads down to the harbor, where the scene changes dramatically. A jumble of fishing shacks, small houses, and wooden piers stands out over the harbor on tall stilts. A twelve-foot tide often barrels in here during bad weather, so buildings have to be up high and well-protected from the surf. The island lost its only restaurant several years ago to one such tide. A large granite pier where the ferry docks is often piled high with lobster traps, buoys, and seining equipment.

By nine o'clock in the morning the harbor is pretty deserted, the lobster boats and fishermen having long since set out to work their traps. Lobstering is the main industry here, and even many of the young children have their own boats and traps to tend.

Lobstering is the main industry here, and even many of the young children have their own boats and traps to tend.

Providing places to eat at the harbor are a small store that is open about four hours a day, a lunch wagon serving hot dogs and Cokes, and, during the summer, a **farmers' market** that sells locally grown garden and farm products. Cait Bunker, the island's real estate agent, chamber of commerce, and all-around tour guide, also helps run the market and sells her wonderful goat's-milk fudge and cheese here.

There are two sandy beaches on the island, one at each end (check the water temperature before you plunge in!), and lots of woodland paths for exploring. Matinicus is particularly popular with bird watchers, as many species have been sighted here. The Atlantic puffin nests on Matinicus Rock, along with black quillemots, arctic terns, and petrels (the bird that seems to walk on water), and there are often special **bird-watching expeditions** to see them. The Maine Audubon Society calls Matinicus Rock "Maine's most famous sea bird colony." The Coast Guard maintains a **lighthouse** on the island, and if they're not too busy when you arrive, you may get to tour the lighthouse.

The Maine Audubon Society calls Matinicus Rock "Maine's most famous sea bird colony."

The population of Matinicus increases to about two hundred in the summer, and there are usually several cottages for rent to vacationers. Cait Bunker also keeps a list of people on the island who will provide overnight accommodations. Albert Bunker, Cait's uncle, is available to conduct sightseeing trips to Matinicus Rock, and you usually can hire a teenager with his or her own boat for a fishing trip or visit to Criehaven.

Criehaven is just a mile away. While it was once a thriving fishing and farming village, the population has dwindled to only a few summer residents and people who go there to fish. On the charts this island is called Ragged, or as salty fishermen say, "Ragged Ass," which is a corruption of the Abnaki Indian name Racketash, meaning "island rocks." Ever since the 1870s when Robert Crie, a native of Matinicus, bought most of the land on the island and parceled it out almost exclusively to relatives, setting himself up as monarch (he was called "King Crie"), it has been called Criehaven. From 1880 until he died in 1901, Crie owned and farmed most of the acreage of the island. He had a large fishing business with salting and packing facilities and even began a lumbering operation. After his death most of his children sold their land and left the island. No one lives on the island during the winter any longer, and no ferry service or public accommodations of any kind are available.

The small island communities of Matinicus and Criehaven — the two most remote on the Maine coast — are serviced by the **Maine Seacoast Mission** throughout the year. Since 1905, the mission has dedicated itself to serving the religious, spiritual, and physical needs of people in remote coastal areas. Aboard the *Sunbeam*, dubbed "God's Tugboat," ministers are sent to the islands to conduct religious and social services for villages too small to support full-time ministers. Among the things the mission has accomplished over the years have been helping islanders get postal services, establishing schools and tutors (particularly for lighthouse keepers' children), setting up a large lending library, and continuing a very popular Christmas program that reaches more than two thousand children on many of the islands. One of the mission's more important functions includes the invaluable medical and emergency services it provides during times of crisis.

A one-room schoolhouse accommodates the children among Matinicus' seventy-five year-round residents.

A visit to these faraway islands gives you a deep appreciation of the tenacity of Matinicus islanders. As Donna Rogers, who has lived on the island for more than thirty years, says, "I guess what Matinicus offers most is her stubborn refusal to keep up completely with the rest of the world."

As Donna Rogers, who has lived on the island for more than thirty years, says, "I guess what Matinicus offers most is her stubborn refusal to keep up completely with the rest of the world."

ACCESS

ROCKLAND. Directions: Take I-95 (Maine Turnpike) to exit 9 and follow Route 1 north to Rockland center.

MAINE STATE FERRY SERVICE. Directions: Follow Route 1 through the center of Rockland, and the ferry dock is on your right. **Season:** Year-round (ferry to Matinicus only once a month). **Admission:** Charged. **Telephone:** (207) 594-5543.

CAPTAIN ALBERT BUNKER. For information regarding charter service to Matinicus, write to Captain Bunker at Matinicus, ME 04851, or call (207) 366-3737.

STONINGTON FLYING SERVICE. Directions: From Rockland (Route 1) turn right onto South Main Street (Route 73) and continue out toward Owls Head, following signs to Knox County Airport. Take a left turn onto Ash Point Road, where the Stonington Flying Service hangar is located. **Season:** Year-round. **Admission:** Charged. **Telephone:** (207) 596-6211.

CHAMBER OF COMMERCE. For further information about accommodations on Matinicus write to Caitlin Owen Bunker, Matinicus, ME 04851, or call (207) 366-3443.

OTHER ISLANDS

Although it may require an extra measure of curiosity, patience, and energy to get to these islands, you'll be richly rewarded for your efforts.

As you travel farther north through Maine toward the Canadian border along Route 1, towns and villages become fewer and farther apart and great stretches of pine forest block most of the vast panoramic view of the ocean. To catch a glimpse of the ocean — and more often than not, to catch a ferry to your island destination — you'll have to leave the main highway far behind and traverse a number of the slim, jagged peninsulas that extend for several miles from the mainland.

The Cranberry, Swans, and Frenchboro islands, for instance, are reached by crossing a bridge to Mount Desert Island and driving the full sixteen-mile length of the island to its southernmost tip and the ferry landing. Mount Desert Island, known since the late 1800s as an outstanding resort area, is the largest island off the coast of Maine. It also has the highest point along the Atlantic coast, Cadillac Mountain.

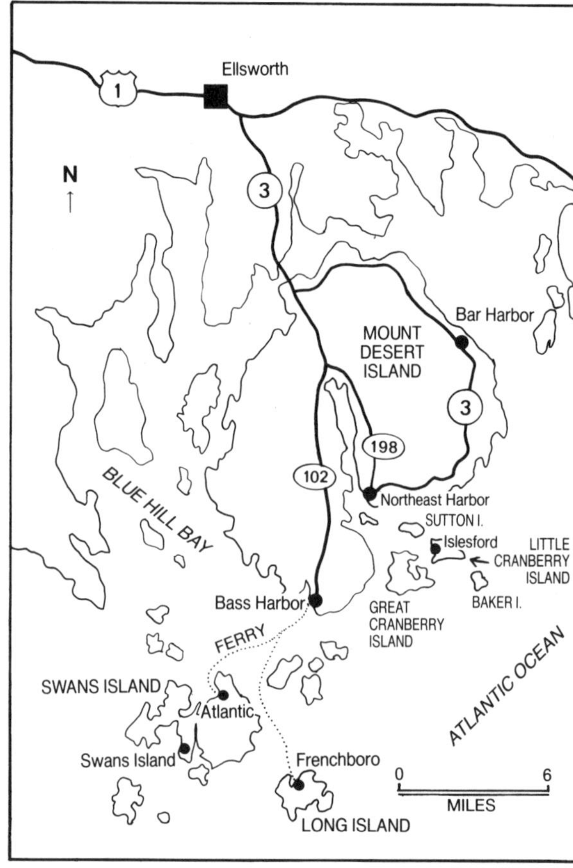

Mount Desert Island, the Cranberry Isles, Swans Island, and Frenchboro

The final and farthest stop on your island-hopping adventure, Campobello, will take you through even more remote and sparsely settled country, right to the Canadian border.

Although it may require an extra measure of curiosity, patience, and energy to get to these islands, you'll be richly rewarded for your efforts. You'll discover not only some of the most pristine and beautiful spots in New England, but also locations that offer almost unlimited activities.

Mount Desert Island

Mount Desert Island is one of the most visited islands in the United States. But you don't have to worry about bumping elbows with anyone here. The island, encompassing **Acadia National Park,** measures slightly more than one hundred square miles, making it the third largest in the country. It has eighteen mountains, including **Cadillac,** the highest point along the Atlantic coast, as well as at least twenty-six freshwater lakes and numerous ponds, streams, coves, and harbors. And as if that weren't enough, there's the magnificent **Somes Sound,** the only true fjord on the East Coast, which almost divides the island in two. All of these great natural resources, to which thousands of visitors flock each year, are easily accessible — and *free.*

CAROLYN J. CASEY

Thunder Hole is a particular favorite among children.

After driving across a small causeway from Trenton, Maine (where there is also a small airport served by **Bar Harbor Airlines**), your first stop will be the **Visitor's Information Center.** Here you can acquaint yourself with the almost mind-boggling array of activities available on the island as well as lodging and restaurants. (All the attractions discussed in this chapter are easily located on maps provided free at the information center.)

Armed with a fistful of complimentary maps and brochures from the information center, you might want to start your visit with a drive along the **Park Loop Road,** a twenty-mile loop around the southeastern portion of the island. Children particularly love to stop at **Thunder Hole**, where the sea rushes into a deep crevice in the rocks, sending up a giant spray of water and a loud "BOOM" that sounds like thunder. Another favorite with kids is listening to the "bubbles" as the water rolls over the stones (or bare toes) in **Bubble Pond.** Both locations are shown on park maps.

Cadillac Mountain, the highest point along the Atlantic coast, affords terrific views.

A stop at the **Wild Gardens of Acadia,** where all the native plants of the area are labeled and grouped around gravel paths, is not only lovely and fragrant but educational as well. **Abbe Museum,** filled with Indian artifacts and local history exhibits, is also located on the Loop Road, as is the entrance to the drive up Cadillac Mountain. The road for the 1,530-foot climb is remarkably well-engineered and constructed, making the drive up and down an easy one. The grade is gradual, and many parking areas along the way provide terrific views.

These carriage paths were conceived and financed by John D. Rockefeller, Jr., one of the summer residents of the island in the early 1900s when the island was, indeed, a haven for the very rich.

More than one hundred twenty miles of trails meander through the park, ranging from short, level walks along the beach to the steep **Precipice Trail.** A network of more than fifty miles of carriage paths (woodland paths where only hikers, bicyclists, and horseback riders are allowed) lead along the banks of beaver-dammed brooks, through pine-drenched forests, and over old, hand-cut granite bridges. These carriage paths were conceived and financed by John D. Rockefeller, Jr., one of the summer residents of the island in the early 1900s when the island was, indeed, a haven for the very rich. Rockefeller, along with other prominent summer residents such as the Morgans, Astors, and Vanderbilts, began buying and setting aside this land to preserve it for the future. The result of their efforts is the 34,450-acre Acadia National Park, the only national park in the country completely donated from private sources.

During the winter months, many of the carriage roads and trails serve as paths for cross-country skiing and, in a few cases, snowmobiling. Ice fishing and winter hiking also are popular, and for the truly hardy outdoor sport, **Blackwoods Campgrounds** is open all winter long.

The **Eagle Lake Loop Road** is specially graded for bicycles, and there are several bike rental shops on the island. Mopeds, including the fancy Mercedes-Benz models with all the "extras," also are available for rent and are perfect for some of the hilly roads. **Wildwood Stables** offers guided horseback trips and wagon rides, for which the carriage roads are ideal.

A wonderful aid for travelers, particularly those who prefer to enjoy the view from the comfort of a car, is the **Tape Tour,** which describes the geological origin, ecology, and history of the park and contains instructions for making the drive around Acadia. This Tape Tour covers approximately fifty-six miles, including Cadillac Mountain, Somes Sound, and all the major attractions, and can be enjoyed in four to six hours at your own pace. You can rent a cassette player and rent or buy a tape at the information center.

Boating and water activities of all kinds are available, including narrated cruises for sightseeing and whale watching, seabird cruises, fishing and sailing charters, boat rentals, and ferry service to several islands. A unique experience for the whole family is a **lobster fishing trip** aboard the *Aunt Elsie*. Not only will you get to see firsthand how lobsters and crabs are hauled in from the bottom of the sea, but also some of the catch will be cooked right onboard for your sampling pleasure.

Not only will you get to see firsthand how lobsters and crabs are hauled in from the bottom of the sea, but also some of the catch will be cooked right onboard for your sampling pleasure.

Maps for self-guided tours are plentiful, but there is also an excellent selection of tours and nature walks led by park naturalists. Bird Walks, Discovery Walks, and Mushroom Talks are just a few of the popular ones. And the more adventurous visitor can go on an evening Night Prowl or Beaver Watch to experience the forest community after dark.

Bar Harbor, known in the early days as Eden, is the largest town on the island and the center of much activity. Many shops, motels, guesthouses, restaurants, and yachting facilities are located here. The movie theater in town is handy for rainy days, but an even better bet is the **Natural History Museum** just outside Bar Harbor on Route 3. This is a hands-on museum that encourages active participation by the whole family in activities such as

One lifelong resident stated flatly, "We don't ca-ah how you pronounce it, long as you say somethin' nice — and don't mention the fog!"

piecing together a giant whale skeleton. The **Mount Desert Oceanarium** in the town of Southwest Harbor is another excellent "touch, feel, taste, hear, and smell" experience for anyone interested in learning all about Maine sea life.

Accommodations on the island fit every pocketbook, from free camping to the exclusive **Claremont Hotel** (on whose green velvet lawn the annual nine-wicket croquet classic is held). July and August are, of course, peak times, and you often have to book reservations at the more popular places well in advance. Some campgrounds operate on a first-come/first-served basis, but others require reservations. A particularly nice moderately priced inn is **The Moorings,** located on Shore Road in Southwest Harbor. The location (facing the harbor) can't be beat, and along with cozy, comfortable rooms, you will always find fresh orange juice, coffee, and doughnuts waiting for you, no matter how early you get up in the morning. The adjoining restaurant, with big windows overlooking the harbor, is very nice at any time of day.

Mount Desert is also the jumping-off place for several other islands, particularly The Cranberry Isles and Swans Island, which are well worth investigating.

French explorer Samuel de Champlain named the island *"L'Isle des Monts Deserts"* in 1604 for its craggy, treeless peaks. But there is still some confusion and much disagreement about the correct pronunciation of the name. While most people pronounce it "dessert" (as in chocolate pudding), others insist on saying "desert" (as in Sahara). Some people ignore the debate altogether, and one lifelong resident stated flatly, "We don't ca-ah how you pronounce it, long as you say somethin' nice — and don't mention the fog!"

ACCESS

MOUNT DESERT ISLAND AND ACADIA NATIONAL PARK. Directions: From Route 1 take Route 3 at Ellsworth, crossing the Mount Desert Narrows to Hull's Cove. The Visitor's Information Center is on your right. The center is open from May 1 through October 31, and a 15-minute film on the island is shown regularly throughout each day. For further information write to the Superintendent, Acadia National Park, Bar Harbor, ME 04609.

BAR HARBOR. Directions: From the information center continue southeast on Route 3 to downtown Bar Harbor and the waterfront.

WILDWOOD STABLES. Directions: Located on the southern tip of Jordan Pond on the Park Loop Road. **Season:** July and August. **Telephone:** (207) 276-5091.

AUNT ELSIE. **Directions:** Approaching Bar Harbor on Route 3, turn left at the first traffic light onto West Street. Follow West Street to the Golden Anchor Pier, where the sightseeing lobster boat *Aunt Elsie* is tied up. **Season:** Mid-May to mid-October. **Admission:** Charged. **Telephone:** (207) 288-9505.

NATURAL HISTORY MUSEUM. Directions: On Route 3 one-half mile west of Bar Harbor. **Season:** Year-round. **Admission:** Charged. **Telephone:** (207) 288-5051.

MOUNT DESERT OCEANARIUM. Directions: From the information center take Route 102 to Southwest Harbor. Turn left onto Clark Point Road and proceed to the waterfront, where the oceanarium is located. **Season:** Mid-May to mid-October. **Admission:** Charged. **Telephone:** (207) 244-7330.

THE MOORINGS. Directions: From the information center, take Route 102 south to Southwest Harbor. Turn onto Route 102A, Shore Road, at Manset. The inn and restaurant are on the left overlooking the harbor. **Season:** Mid-May to mid-October. **Telephone:** (207) 244-5523.

BAR HARBOR CHAMBER OF COMMERCE. Municipal Building, Bar Harbor, ME 04629; (207) 288-5103.

The Cranberry Isles

Don't expect to find cranberries on the Cranberry Isles — any more than you might expect to find hogs on Hog Island, potatoes on Potato Island, or turnips on Turnip Island. That's just the way it is on Maine islands; most of the island names have long since lost their original meanings.

There used to be cranberries here, of course, millions of them in earlier days when cranberry bogs flourished on the island. But now fishing is the main industry, as the enormous stacks of lobster traps lining the docks and front yards around the island will attest.

One thing you will find here is a gem of a restaurant right on the dock of Islesford (Little Cranberry Island). It's called, appropriately, **Islesford Dock Restaurant.** You can dine in the large, rustic dining room or the smaller, brighter, newly added lounge. From both you'll get a panoramic view of Mount Desert Island and a friendly feeling of informality. And while you have a choice of sev-

All the bread and pastries are homemade, and most of the vegetables and herbs are grown on the island.

So popular is the Islesford Dock Restaurant that the ferry from Mount Desert Island makes a special dinner run there each evening.

eral gourmet specialties, lobster Newburg, or charcoal-broiled steaks and chops, the chef also prepares Down East fare, as well as children's favorites, to order. All the bread and pastries are homemade, and most of the vegetables and herbs are grown on the island.

So popular is this place for its food, lounge, and sunset view that a special ferry trip takes passengers from the town of Northeast Harbor on Mount Desert Island out to Islesford and back each evening just for dinner. The regular ferry also makes a special stop at the restaurant's landing dock each night on its last run to be sure no one is left behind. And it's a good thing too. Except for an occasional bed and breakfast place, there are no overnight accommodations on this island or on any of the other Cranberries.

The Cranberries are a group of five islands — Great Cranberry, Little Cranberry (better known as Islesford), Sutton, Baker, and Bear — lying just a few miles out from the busy waterfront of Northeast Harbor. They're small islands, with Great Cranberry being the largest, about two miles long and a mile wide. Little Cranberry is about half that size, and Sutton, Baker, and Bear are smaller still. Bear Island is only big enough for a lighthouse and is not open to visitors. When a local lobsterman was asked recently if there were any bears on the island, he matter-of-factly answered, "Ain't seen none lately." Actually, the island is said to have been named many years ago by someone who thought it was shaped like the head of a bear.

If you take the Nature Cruise aboard the Sea Princess, *you'll get to view, close-up, an osprey nesting site on Sutton and seals and cormorants sunning on nearby rocks and ledges.*

Sutton Island is a small private community of summer homes, and the only uninvited visitors tolerated are osprey, cormorants, and harbor seals. If you take the **Nature Cruise** aboard the *Sea Princess,* you'll get to view, close-up, an osprey nesting site on Sutton and seals and cormorants sunning on nearby rocks and ledges. For many years Sutton was the summer home of one of Maine's favorite writers, Rachel Field. Her novel *Time Out of Mind* was inspired by her summers on Sutton, and another book, *God's Pocket,* focuses on the history of a colorful family that lived on Great Cranberry Island.

Great and Little Cranberry are the only Cranberries that have year-round communities — fewer than one hundred people on each. Each has a one-room schoolhouse (kindergarten through eighth grade) and a country store that doubles as a community information center. Each also has a take-out food service (summer only), gift shop, some interesting old churches, and some good roads for biking and walking.

Another special feature on Little Cranberry is the **Islesford Historical Museum,** which is open daily from June through September. For many years summer resident William Otis Sawtelle, a Haverford College professor, collected history and artifacts of the island. He amassed genealogical records that document the island's early history, many tools and household items, furniture, china, pictures, maps, and many maritime relics such as the figureheads from several ships. These are now housed in an attractive brick building close to the dock and are maintained by Acadia National Park.

Most of **Baker Island's** one hundred acres is part of Acadia National Park. During the summer a special daily **cruise** to the island is available. The four-and-a-half-hour cruise, directed and narrated by a park ranger, takes participants around the island to look at the many unusual plants, animals, and geological formations that cannot be found anywhere else in this area. An offshore pile of huge slabs of granite called the Dance Floor is one such interesting sight. You'll also get to observe several seal and osprey nesting areas on the way out to Baker.

ACCESS

NORTHEAST HARBOR. Directions: From the information booth at the entrance to Mount Desert Island take Route 198 south to Northeast Harbor. Turn left onto Sea Street to Municipal Pier at the Sea Street Marina. Free parking.

MAIL BOAT AND FERRY SERVICE (*Sea Queen*). Directions: *Sea Queen* is located at Municipal Pier, Northeast Harbor. **Season:** Year-round. **Admission:** Charged. **Telephone:** (207) 244-3575.

ISLESFORD DOCK RESTAURANT. Directions: Islesford Ferry leaves from the Sea Street Pier in Northeast Harbor. Call the restaurant for reservations and the ferry schedule. **Season:** June to September (lunch, dinner, and take-out). **Telephone:** (207) 244-3177.

ISLESFORD HISTORICAL CRUISE (*Sea Princess*). Directions: *Sea Princess* is located at the Municipal Pier, Northeast Harbor. **Season:** June through September. **Admission:** Charged. **Telephone:** (207) 244-3575.

NATURE CRUISE AND BAKER ISLAND CRUISE (Islesford Ferry). Directions: Islesford Ferry departs from the Municipal Pier in Northeast Harbor. **Season:**

The Islesford Historical Museum on Little Cranberry Island houses an interesting collection of island memorabilia, including old tools, furnishings, and photographs.

Mid-June to Labor Day. **Admission:** Charged. **Telephone:** (207) 244-3366.

ISLESFORD HISTORICAL MUSEUM. Directions: Islesford Ferry leaves from the Sea Street Pier in Northeast Harbor (several round trips a day). The museum is located within a short walking distance of the ferry landing. **Admission:** Free. **Telephone (Acadia National Park Information):** (207) 288-3338.

Swans Island

Some islands, unlike the Cranberries, which are so invitingly close to shore and have frequent ferry runs, are decidedly difficult to get to. And being so, they have remained virtually unspoiled and unchanged over the years. Swans Island and Frenchboro (Long Island) are two such islands. Because they are so far off the beaten path, even the Victorian summer rusticators bypassed them for the more accessible islands.

Swans Island and Frenchboro have the look and feel of typical Maine fishing villages with little or no acquiescence to the tourist trade. But that's not to say day-trippers should stay away. On the contrary, Swans Island in particular offers an abundance of vacationer opportunities: miles of wonderfully scenic roads for biking; two excellent public beaches (one, Fine Sand Beach, has, indeed, the finest sand you'll find on any New England island beach); a surprisingly contemporary restaurant,

TOM HINDMAN

Water meets land at Hockomock Head, Burnt Coat Harbor, Swans Island.

The Bridge, which features "classic dining"; a fairly large market with a deli take-out section; several gift shops; a Natural History Museum; and an attractive gallery and art supply store where local artists display and sell their work.

Swans Island (it is sometimes spelled "Swan's" Island) also boasts one of the more colorful histories of any Maine island. James Swan, an extraordinary entrepreneur, bought the island in 1786 with great plans for developing his own little empire. He set about building a lumbermill, a gristmill, and a mansion for himself, and he offered one hundred acres to every family who would settle on the island.

The Swans Island Methodist Church, built in 1888, is one of four churches on the island.

But Swan himself, a former Son of Liberty who had participated in the Boston Tea Party and the Battle of Bunker Hill, never got to live on the island. A man of strong principles, he spent more than twenty years in a debtors' prison in France rather than pay a debt he insisted he did not owe. He finally was released in 1830, but died shortly thereafter, before he was able to return to the island. His wife and four children never moved to the island either, preferring instead to live in their fashionable home on Beacon Hill in Boston.

To this day, however, most of the approximately three hundred fifty people who live on the island year-round are direct descendants of those early pioneers who took advantage of Swan's original land offer. And while the lumbermill and the gristmill are long gone, the fishing shacks surrounding Burnt Coat Harbor and the miles of lobster buoys stretching out across Penobscot Bay are evidence of a prosperous fishing enterprise here.

Swan himself, a former Son of Liberty who had participated in the Boston Tea Party and the Battle of Bunker Hill, never got to live on the island.

Swans Island is actually only four miles out to sea, but to get to the ferry that takes you there you must first drive the full length of Mount Desert Island to the tiny village of Bass Harbor on the island's southernmost tip. The ferry trip takes about forty minutes aboard the twelve-car *Everett Libby,* and during the peak of the season cars are backed up in line for hours waiting to get on or off the island. While the wait may be frustrating, most islanders are adamant about not wanting to increase the runs or the size of the ferry for fear of creating more traffic on the island. In recent years more and more people have discovered Swans Island, creating a worrisome real estate boom and skyrocketing land costs.

The smart traveler will take a bike to the island, as the ferry landing in Atlantic is several miles from most points of interest. Swans is fairly large, being twelve miles from end to end. But it has such an irregular shape that in some parts, such as **The Carrying Place,** it measures only twenty yards across. This area was so named because Indians used it as a short cut, carrying their canoes across the narrow expanse of land to get from one side of the bay to the other.

The erratic shape of the island divides it into thirds, creating three separate little villages. Atlantic is on the northern shore, where the ferry lands, and Minturn and Swans Island Village nestle on the east and west sides of Burnt Coat Harbor. The name Burnt Coat is said to be a corruption of *Brûle-Côte* (brown coast), which was the name Champlain gave to it when he first sighted it.

Most of today's Swans Island residents are descendants of people who accepted James Swan's offer to move here in the late 1700s.

Tourist attractions are spread out around the island, making for convenient stops during your walking or biking exploration. **Ocean Notions,** run by Priscilla Lunt (a surname you'll hear quite often on both Frenchboro and Swans), is a small gift shop stocked with hand-knits and other items made by local craftspeople. It also carries *The Swans Island Cookbook* and the *Frenchboro Cookbook,* both chock-full of wonderful Down East recipes. **The Imagesmith,** run by award-winning photographer Tom Hindman and decorated with his work and that of other islanders, is a great place for browsing and buying. A large selection of photographs, watercolors, and oils depicting local scenes is for sale.

Two particularly picturesque spots for enjoying the view and picnicking are **Hockomock Head,** where an old but now automated lighthouse marks the entrance to Burnt Coat Harbor, and **Quarry Pond,** on the opposite side of the harbor in Minturn, offering freshwater swimming in an old granite quarry with steppingstones leading down to the pond.

Swans Island Museum and Library, housed in a single building, is next to the ferry landing. Along with a collection of island artifacts including Indian arrowheads, photographs, books, tools, and toys, you'll see a room furnished as an early American bedroom from an island home during the early settlement days. The museum and library usually are open on Saturday afternoons year-round and also on various days throughout the summer.

One of the more interesting places to visit is the **Natural History Museum and Gift Shop** out on The Carrying Place. Run by Marge Bailey and Maili Currier, it is small but is filled with exhibits of all sorts of unusual sea creatures swimming in tanks or preserved in jars (these exhibits change with the season), along with island flora and fauna. The museum also has a collection of hand-hooked chair pads, piano-bench pads, stair treads, and wall hangings, most of which have island themes such as starfish, shells, sunsets, and island flowers. You can get a copy of the *History of Swan's Island, Maine,* written in 1898 by H.W. Small, which is filled with amusing tidbits about town meetings and legislation ("1866, Voted to tax dogs $5.") and makes for interesting reading. You can also buy a very good but inexpensive map and guide to the island here.

Maili Currier also runs the **Swans Island Guest House** in Minturn, and Marge's mother, **Peg Bailey,** is the person to contact if you want to rent a vacation house for a week or two. The only other island accommodations are found at **Alberta Buswell's Guest House.** The Buswells, who live out on Long Cove in Minturn, rent rooms in their home as well as a few small cabins.

Other than the Tuesday evening lecture series at the local library, community hymn sings, and church suppers, life is fairly quiet here.

Other than the Tuesday evening lecture series at the local library, community hymn sings, and church suppers (there are four churches on the island), life is fairly quiet here. **Sunday breakfasts** at the Odd Fellows Hall are highlights of the summer season and are anticipated by islanders and visitors alike.

ACCESS

BASS HARBOR AND FERRY. Directions: From the information booth at the entrance to Mount Desert Island take Route 198 south to Somesville. From Somesville take Route 102 south through Southwest Harbor, continuing south and following Swans Island Ferry signs to Bass Harbor and the ferry landing. **Season:** Year-round. **Admission:** Charged. **Telephone:** (207) 244-3254.

THE GENERAL STORE. Directions: From the ferry landing in Atlantic take a right at the end of the road onto Main Road. Follow it for about two miles until you reach Main Road to Minturn, on your left. The store is about a mile up on the right. **Season:** Year-round. **Telephone:** (207) 526-4200. **Note:** Most of the roads do not have names other than Main Road to Minturn or Main Road to Swans Island Village, etc.

THE BRIDGE. Directions: From the ferry landing in Atlantic take a right at the end of the road onto Main Road to Swans Island Village. The restaurant is on your left. **Season:** Mid-June through Labor Day (dinner only). **Telephone:** (207) 526-4343.

OCEAN NOTIONS. Directions: From the ferry landing in Atlantic take a right onto Main Road to Swans Island

Village. The gift shop is on your left. **Season:** Mid-June through Christmas.

THE IMAGESMITH. Directions: From the ferry landing in Atlantic take a right at the end of the road onto Main Road to Swans Island Village. The shop is on your left. **Season:** Year-round. **Telephone:** (207) 526-4130.

SWANS ISLAND MUSEUM AND LIBRARY. Directions: Directly across the road from the ferry landing. **Season:** Saturday afternoon year-round and various other days during the summer. **Admission:** Free (donations appreciated).

NATURAL HISTORY MUSEUM AND GIFT SHOP. Directions: From the ferry landing in Atlantic take Main Road to Swan's Island Village. Just after passing the Odd Fellows Hall (large building on right), turn right to The Carrying Place. The museum is on your left. **Season:** June to mid-October. **Admission:** Free. **Telephone:** (207) 526-4122.

SWANS ISLAND GUEST HOUSE. Directions: From the ferry landing in Atlantic take a right onto the Main Road for about two miles. Turn left onto Main Road to Minturn for about two miles, and the guesthouse is on your right. **Season:** Year-round. **Telephone:** (207) 526-4350.

PEG BAILEY, REALTOR (Vacation House Rentals). The Carrying Place, Swans Island, ME 04685; (207) 526-4122.

ALBERTA BUSWELL'S GUEST HOUSE. Directions: From the ferry landing in Atlantic take a right onto the Main Road for about two miles. Turn left onto the Main Road to Minturn and follow it almost to the end. Buswell's is on your right. **Season:** Year-round. **Telephone:** (207) 526-4127.

Frenchboro (Long Island)

In 1983 the forty or so residents who make up the small settlement on this twenty-five-hundred-acre island petitioned the state of Maine for funds to shore up their declining population.

If you've ever dreamed of leaving the mainland behind forever and settling down in a picturesque little fishing village out in the middle of the sea, Frenchboro — Long Island — may be just the place for you. Frenchboro, in fact, *wants* you.

In 1983 the forty or so residents who make up the small settlement on this twenty-five-hundred-acre island petitioned the State of Maine for funds to shore up their declining population. The funds, which were granted in 1985, enable the town to offer low-interest loans to young couples of child-bearing age who agree to work and live on the island year-round. While this offer hardly compares to the one James Swan made to settlers on Swans

Island more than two hundred years ago (one hundred acres and a guaranteed job), so far more than a hundred people have responded to Frenchboro's proposition. Local administrators carefully interview prospective candidates to let them know that while Frenchboro may look like a picture-post-card setting, its way of life is not for everyone. Still, Frenchboro officials hope to recruit at least ten families to settle on the island in the next four or five years.

Frenchboro is only five miles from Swans Island, and although linked to it in many ways (most of the people on the two islands are related to one another), there's a definite feeling of stepping back in time as you enter Frenchboro's small horseshoe-shaped harbor. A scattering of weathered houses nestles into a hillside backed by dense and uninhabited woods of spruce and fir. The spire of a small white church is reflected alongside rustic fishing shacks and long-legged piers in the blue-black water. While television antennas and utility poles are not dominant, the island does have electricity (since 1950) and recently received telephone service.

REBECCA J. LUNT

A visit to Frenchboro is like a step back in time.

At the turn of the century, the town of Frenchboro, which is the only settlement on the island, was a small but thriving fishing community. Even though the population never exceeded two hundred, the town built a fine school for its then sixty or so students. But as with so many other Maine islands, when fishing declined, families left, too. When the enrollment at the local two-room schoolhouse dropped to two students a few years ago, the State of Maine threatened to cut off aid. The islanders rallied together, inviting more than a dozen foster children from the mainland to come out and live on the island. The children settled in well, living with island families until they were ready for high school and had to return to the mainland. Since then, a few have returned to the island as permanent members of the community.

Because islanders own most of the available property, Frenchboro is one of the few island communities that does not have much of a summer population. A large portion of the island, however, is owned by a nonresident, Margaret Rockefeller Dulaney, daughter of David Rockefeller, who donated a fifty-five-acre parcel of land to be used for the one-acre house lots offered to new settlers.

Few, if any, jobs are available, but there are plenty of opportunities for the resourceful person. The island badly needs certain commercial facilities, such as a general store. At present the Maine State Ferry stops at the island only twice a week, necessitating an expensive overnight trip to the mainland for islanders to do their shopping. If more full-time residents move to Frenchboro, islanders hope the state will increase its ferry service.

While it is a difficult place to get to and no meals or lodging is available, Frenchboro is still an interesting and beautiful island to explore. A paved road runs along the harbor, with several dirt roads and paths leading through the woods. You'll be greeted along the way by any number of friendly deer that can be coaxed into feeding out of your hand. If you happen to be on the island in late July or early August, you might ask directions to the "bog," where more than an acre of rare pale lavender orchids (Pogonia) bloom in profusion.

You'll be greeted along the way by any number of friendly deer that can be coaxed into feeding out of your hand.

The island has a **historical society** and a small museum (in the basement of Rebecca Lunt's home), where island memorabilia can be viewed and island-made crafts purchased. Each summer, sometime in August, the historical society and the local church hold an annual all-day fair to raise money for both institutions, and the state ferry provides extra boat trips to the island for the occasion.

ACCESS

MAINE STATE FERRY SERVICE. Directions: From the Visitor's Information Booth at the entrance to Mount Desert Island take Route 198 south to Somesville. From Somesville take Route 102 south through Southwest Harbor. Continue south and follow the signs to the ferry landing in Bass Harbor. A single trip, 2 days a week, leaves from Bass Harbor on Mount Desert Island. Call for time and schedules. **Admission:** Charged. **Season:** Year-round. **Telephone:** (207) 244-3254.

FRENCHBORO MAIL BOAT. Directions: From the ferry landing go half a mile to the first intersection and turn right onto Main Road. Swans Island Village is about 2 miles away. Just past the village take a left turn (short road) to Kent's Wharf. The mail boat leaves from Kent's Wharf in Swans Island Village 4 days a week, making a round trip (staying only about 15 minutes on the island). It generally leaves in the early afternoon, but check at the post office for the exact time of departure. **Season:** Year-round. **Admission:** Charged.

FRENCHBORO HISTORICAL SOCIETY AND MUSEUM. Plans for construction of a permanent home for the society's collection of historic documents and photographs are underway. Contact Vivian Lunt, Frenchboro, ME 04653.

FDR loved to paddle around Campobello's beautiful Lake Glensevern in this birch bark canoe, now displayed on the back porch of the Roosevelts' former summer cottage.

Campobello

It is most fitting that the memory of so gallant and industrious an American [as FDR] should be honored on the Canadian Island which he loved.

Her Majesty Queen Elizabeth the Queen Mother
at the opening of Roosevelt-Campobello
International Park on July 13, 1967.

The Webster-Ashburton Treaty of 1842, establishing the international boundary between Canada and the United States, may have assigned the island of Campobello to New Brunswick, Canada, but to the thousands of American visitors who make pilgrimages here each year, the island belongs to them.

The nine-mile-long and three-mile-wide Campobello Island lies only two hundred fifty yards from Lubec, Maine ("the easternmost city in the U.S."), and is, in its own right, a small fishing community with a population of about twelve hundred. But every summer approximately 125,000 visitors cross the Franklin D. Roosevelt Memorial Bridge, taking a sentimental journey to the former summer home and "beloved island" of the thirty-second president of the United States.

The Roosevelt summer home and grounds are the centerpiece of the twenty-six-hundred-acre **Roosevelt-Campobello International Park,** jointly administered by the United States and Canada.

Like so many other islands, Campobello was discovered by wealthy Americans during the Gild-

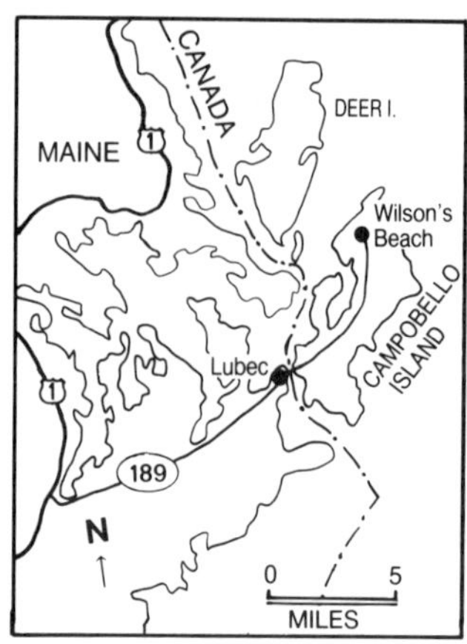

Campobello Island

ed Age, when no island, it seemed, was too far north to be left untouched by their quest for the perfect summer resort. When a group of American businessmen purchased a good portion of the island in the late 1880s, they developed the southern end into an exclusive summer colony and began an intense advertising campaign to attract residents. Several large hotels were built offering "all the comforts of a refined home" and proclaiming such healthful features as "absolute relief from hay fever" and the restorative effects of "baths of fog"!

The James Roosevelts were among the early families who built a home here. Their young son, Franklin, came here every summer, learning to swim, fish, and navigate a boat through the dangerous Lubec Narrows. It was on Campobello that he met his future wife, Eleanor, and where, after marriage, they returned each summer with their own growing family. Their fourth child, Franklin D. Roosevelt, Jr., was born on Campobello by the light of an oil lamp in a hastily fashioned delivery room of their cottage. (His Canadian birthplace would later prove a stumbling block in his own political career.)

But the Campobello event that most deeply affected the Roosevelt family occurred on an August day in 1921. Franklin, after a full day of sailing, swimming, hiking, and helping to fight a forest fire, plunged into the frigid waters of the Bay of Fundy, which borders the island. He had developed a chill and feelings of fatigue the previous day when he accidentally fell overboard from a fishing boat, but after this second plunge into the bay, the chill returned, and by the following morning, he was running a high temperature. His illness was later diagnosed as infantile paralysis — polio.

It has been said that Roosevelt's "Harvard" accent, which became such a well-known trademark during his Fireside Chats, actually was the distinctive accent of the Campobello fishermen with whom he had a close association throughout his youth.

It left him with severely crippled legs, but in spite of it he was to go on to an unparalleled political career, being elected governor of New York twice and president of the United States four consecutive times. The park, established in the 1960s "as an expression of the close relationship between Canada and the United States," is now open every day from late May to early October.

At the **Reception Center**, an introduction to the island and the Roosevelt family is provided by way of several films shown alternately every hour on the hour. It is only a short walk from the center to the **Roosevelt Cottage**, where visitors can stroll leisurely through the thirty-four rooms (seventeen bedrooms) chock-full of memorabilia such as model ships made by FDR and his children, photographs of the family and important visitors, and FDR's famous felt hat, which sits on a stool in his study. The house is meticulously maintained, and friendly guides are stationed throughout, ready to answer questions or provide interesting information about some of the family belongings.

Most of the furnishings are original, including the wallpaper, rugs, and curtains (in a few cases, reproductions were necessary). The large frame chair used to carry the disabled president about the grounds is here, as is the improvised stretcher his fishermen friends made for him when he first became ill and had to be carried to the boat. The huge megaphone used by Eleanor to call the children for meals still sits by the dining room door, and the boys' bikes, parked out on the back porch, look ready for action. In the living room, furnished in wicker and chintz, the familiar voice of FDR can be heard coming from an old wooden radio. It has been said that Roosevelt's "Harvard" accent, which became such a well-known trademark during his Fireside Chats, actually was the distinctive accent of the Campobello fishermen with whom he had a close association throughout his youth.

The interior furnishings of the Roosevelt cottage have been well preserved.

Besides the house and grounds, the island boasts several other points of interest. **Snug Cove** is where the notorious traitor Benedict Arnold and his wife lived for a while shortly after the American Revolution. **Friar's Head** and the strange rock formation called Old Friar were used by the British fleet as a target for cannon practice in 1814 (substantially reducing the head of the Old Friar). **East Quoddy Light,** a sparkling red and white lighthouse on a prominent point, affords wonderful views of the surrounding sea.

There are innumerable hiking trails, good roads for biking, and swimming at **Herring Cove Beach** and **Lake Glensevern,** a freshwater pond. Also at Herring Cove are a well-equipped camping and picnic area and a nine-hole golf course.

Wilson's Beach, the location of the first English settlement on the island, is now the center of the island's small but active fishing industry. You can buy plenty of fresh and salted fish here as well as what the locals claim to be "the world's best sardines," which are processed in a nearby plant.

The island has a small motel **(Friar's Bay Motor Lodge)** and a few guesthouses, as well as two or three restaurants (all featuring fresh fish, of course). Also, along North Road (one of the main roads) you'll find a grocery store and a few gift shops.

The **Campobello Library and Museum** is housed in the oldest building on the island and displays some of the personal possessions of Captain William Owen, the original "owner" of Campobello Island. Owen received the island as a grant from the governor of Nova Scotia, Lord William Campbell, in 1767. He said that he chose the name Campo Bello (Italian for "beautiful field") "partly complimenting and punning the name of the governor." Some old photographs of the Roosevelt family and the early summer resort days also are on display.

While there is a small medical center on the island, it is interesting to note that because the closest hospital is in Lubec, Maine, many Campobello babies are born in the United States, thus giving parents the right to choose their baby's citizenship either in Canada or the States. Most parents, it is said, tend to be very proud and possessive of the Campobello heritage.

ACCESS

CAMPOBELLO ISLAND. Directions: From Route 1 take Route 189 to Lubec. Cross the Franklin D. Roosevelt Memorial Bridge and proceed to the Canadian Customs Station (no credentials needed). The Visitor's Information Building is just a short distance along the same road, on your right. (Both buildings will be in view after you cross the bridge.) You can pick up a free map that clearly pinpoints all the attractions mentioned in this chapter.

ROOSEVELT-CAMPOBELLO INTERNATIONAL PARK. Directions: Proceed from the Visitor's Information Building about 2 miles to the Visitor's Reception Center. (Entrance sign is on your left.) **Season:** Early May to late October. **Admission:** Free. **Telephone:** (506) 752-2922. **Address:** Executive Secretary, Welshpool, Campobello, New Brunswick, Canada, EOG 3HO.

FRIAR'S BAY MOTOR LODGE. Directions: From the Visitor's Information Building follow North Road to Welshpool past the entrance to Roosevelt-Campobello International Park. The lodge is about 1 mile along on your right. **Season:** May to mid-October. **Telephone:** (506) 752-2056.

CAMPOBELLO LIBRARY AND MUSEUM. Directions: Follow the main road (North Road) from the Visitor's Information Building to Welshpool. The museum is on your left near the pier. **Season:** May to mid-October. **Admission:** Free.

TOURIST INFORMATION CENTER. Campobello Island, New Brunswick, Canada, EOG 3HO; (506) 752-2997.

VERMONT

Autumn is apple picking time at Allenholm Farm in South Hero.

Vermont is the only completely inland New England state. But though it may not have the great Atlantic Ocean lapping at its borders, in the opinion of many it has something far better. The sparkling waters of majestic Lake Champlain stretch approximately one hundred twenty miles along Vermont's western border, constituting more than half the state's boundary with New York.

In 1609 French explorer Samuel de Champlain accompanied a war party of Algonquins down the Richelieu River from Quebec to see for himself the large lake that he was later to describe as "beautiful . . . full of fair islands and of fine countries." After engaging in a bloody battle with the Iroquois along

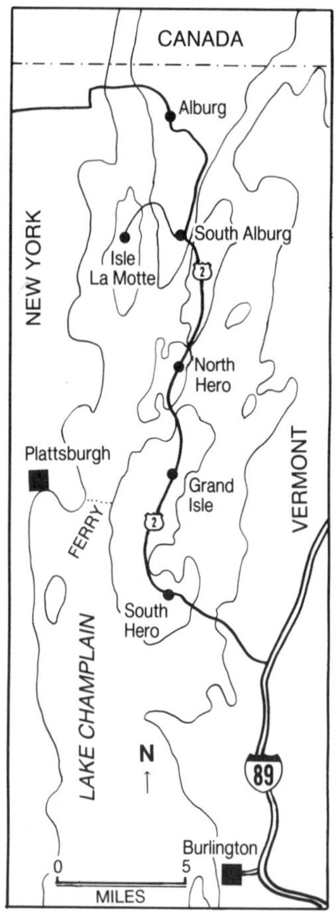

The Islands of Vermont

the way, Champlain promptly changed the name of the great body of water from Sea of the Iroquois to Lake Champlain. And although he was never to return to his lake, at least one of the "fair islands" he stopped at was to be among the first settlements in Vermont.

Grand Isle County comprises the five island towns of South Hero, North Hero, Grand Isle, Alburg, and Isle La Motte, which are linked to one another by a series of causeways and bridges. "The Islands," as they are generally referred to, are connected to mainland Vermont by a mile-long, two-lane highway built over a natural sandbar. They are linked with New York by a ferry, which travels on frequent runs between Grand Isle and Plattsburgh. Alburg, which is actually a peninsula extending down from Canada, is connected to New York by a bridge at Rouses Point.

The islands originally were called the Isles of the Two Heroes in honor of two of the state's famous Green Mountain Boys, Ethan and Ira Allen, who fought in the Revolutionary War. In 1783, their cousin Ebenezer Allen was the first to homestead island land, floating his family, their belongings, and the lumber for a house up the lake from the town of Shelburne. His house still stands in South Hero and is lived in, as are many other early houses, some of them made of stone quarried on the island. Farming is still the main industry, and as you travel the thirty-mile length of the islands you pass field after field of rolling farmland, grazing cows, and apple orchards on either side of the road.

Each summer the islands' combined population of approximately five thousand quintuples with visitors from all over the world. Boating, camping, and fishing head the list of popular sports, but just about every summer activity is available. Fishing remains popular year-round, and the lake is dotted with fishing shanties throughout the winter.

You won't find any fast-food places on the islands, but you won't need them. On any summer weekend you can eat your way across the islands from one fund-raising meal to another. There are roast beef dinners, chicken barbecues, turkey dinners, pancake breakfasts, and any number of potlucks and picnics.

And when it comes to entertainment, that too is homemade: Softball games, symphonies, bike rides, walking tours, readings, a marathon, a triathlon, an air show, craft shows, and auctions are among the attractions you're likely to encounter.

You won't find many indoor activities on the Lake Champlain islands because people here enjoy being outdoors and taking advantage of the natural beauty the islands have to offer.

An excellent map of the Lake Champlain islands, complete with listings of recreational spots, historic sites, lodging, and restaurants, is available free from the chamber of commerce or for a nominal fee at most general stores and gift shops on the islands.

South Hero/Grand Isle

Travelers entering Vermont's island county by passing over the unique **Sand Bar Bridge** from Milton to South Hero are afforded a good introduction to the beauty that lies ahead. The sandbar separates the clear, blue waters of Lake Champlain, which stretch out in a gorgeous panorama on either side as far as the eye can see. The bridge itself sometimes provides the traveler with an unusual experience. Local writer and historian Eloise Hedbor, in writing about the hazards of crossing earlier, cruder sandbar bridges that were usually reclaimed each spring by ice and high water, states, "When the south wind blows in the early winter or drives the breaking ice in the spring, there may still be more than a few days when spray from Lake Champlain freezes on the road surface or forms fantastic sculptures on the guard rails . . . ."

Both the bridge and the main road through the islands have been improved over the years (some natives wish they hadn't!), affording tourists thirty miles of some of the most scenic, unspoiled vistas in Vermont. Mountains rise up on either side of the lake — the Green Mountains on the east and the Adirondacks on the west. This is the area that the French explorers first saw and called *Vert Mont,* meaning "green mountain."

At every bend in the road, lush green farmland thick with cornstalks in the late summer and ripening apple orchards in the early fall fills the broad strips of land along the water's edge.

At every bend in the road, lush green farmland thick with cornstalks in the late summer and ripening apple orchards in the early fall fills the broad strips of land along the water's edge. Huge silver silos glistening in the sun and large herds of grazing Holsteins attest to the preponderance of dairy farming in this region. Nearly eighty percent of the land is in farms, with milk production leading the way, followed by apples and hay.

Allenholm Farm in South Hero, owned and operated by Ray Allen, whose family has been on the island since the late 1700s, has Vermont's oldest commercial orchard. Ray is the largest apple grower in the county and, along with his wife, Pam, represents the younger generation of islanders who combine the best of the past with a modern lifestyle.

Ray bought the farm from his father in 1960 and has increased its size from sixty-five acres to one hundred twenty. At the height of the picking season he employs more than one hundred handpickers, many of whom are homemakers from the surrounding area. "Housewives are used to doing piecework," Ray says, "and they have learned to do things efficiently. There's a skill and an art to picking apples, and you need people who are nimble and well-coordinated." Ray says he has hired some women who have picked as many as one hundred bushels a day each, and one woman "outpicked a whole crew of men with 156 bushels in one day."

Life on Allenholm Farm is not all work. Ray, who flies his own plane and has an airstrip on the farm, hosts the immensely popular **Experimental Aircraft Association's Open House Picnic** each year. Pilots fly in from around the state, and observers are treated (free of charge) to displays of various types of aircraft and some death-defying stunts.

Not far from Allenholm Farm is another spread of beautiful acreage called, appropriately, **Contentment Farm.** Owned by the Yates family for more than thirty years, this is an outstanding riding stable offering trail riding, instruction, pony rides, hay and sleigh rides, boarding, and a tack shop. The farrier at the stables is Peter Yates, who tends horses all over northwestern Vermont and northeastern New York, as well as taking care of the fifty or so horses on the farm. Contentment Farm is owned by Peter's father, Robert, and many members of the family, including aunts, cousins, nieces, and nephews, pitch in to do chores and give lessons. Along with an indoor arena, the farm has trails that wind through the woods, along the lake, and across the meadows.

Guess where these young spectators at Contentment Farm would rather be sitting!

Another interesting stop just down the road from Allenholm Farm is **Island Country Quilts.** In an addition on the back of her home, Irene Falby displays more than four hundred bolts of calico, a collection of quilts (both new and antique), embroidered pillows, baby gifts, and a complete supply of quilting and stenciling materials.

Irene, who is a former president of the Green Mountain Quilters Guild, says, "I came home one night from a meeting about five years ago, woke up

Irene Falby's Island Country Quilts shop has grown every year since she started it in a small room off the back of her house.

my husband, and told him, 'I'm going to open a quilting shop.' " She started in a small room off the back of the house, and the shop has grown every year, she says. About fifty-five to sixty people from the area contribute their handmade work on a consignment basis. Along with giving lessons and lecturing on quilts, Irene repairs antique quilts.

Out along the main road (Route 2) in South Hero is **The Apple Farm Market,** a wonderfully refreshing stop, particularly on a hot day. Just about anything made from apples is sold here, including their famous cider doughnuts. And at their ice cream stand, among the seemingly unlimited variety of treats, you'll find the thirst-quencher to end all thirsts — the cider slush.

Just about everything made from apples is sold here, including their famous cider doughnuts.

As South Hero has the only commercial center to speak of on the islands, you may want to drop in at the **Post and Beam,** the island's only dry-goods store, run by Pam Allen (of Allenholm Farm) and her partner, Mary Sue Tourbille.

Running is a very popular sport in this area, as is exemplified by the **Fun Run.** Whole families turn out for this short race "just for the fun of it." It's held on Saturday mornings from mid-June to the end of August (check the local paper for the schedule) and is open to all at no charge. In addition, the **Green Mountain Island Marathon** is held in South Hero each August. The 26.2-mile course begins and ends on South Street near the house where Clarence H. Demar, a seven-time winner of the Boston Marathon, once lived. The race, which winds through dairy farms and apple orchards, is run under the auspices of the Green Mountain Athletic Association and attracts between two hundred fifty and three hundred runners, from novices to experts. As with most community events on the islands, everyone participates. Islanders cheer runners along the route and offer them swigs of water from their garden hoses. It's a gala event and is considered the number one marathon in the state.

The town of **Grand Isle,** known until 1810 as Middle Hero, shares the same island with South Hero. It is one of the fastest growing towns in Vermont (the population, now 1,244, increased more than fifty-three percent during the 1970s), but it is certainly hard to detect such growth. From Route 2, or even on a side trip down one of the more rural roads, you'll find the landscape dotted with small homes and farms that look as though they have been there forever.

Zigzagging split-rail fences, some of them having been in place for more than two hundred years, follow the roads and cut across farmland and meadows. Weathered to an antique gray, the long cedar rails are balanced on top of each other in such a way that they need nothing more than their own weight to hold them together.

Hostess Mary Rooks introduces visitors to the many fascinating artifacts on display at the Hyde Log Cabin in Grand Isle.

"They were made that way," says Mary Rooks, hostess at the **Hyde Log Cabin,** "so that farmers could easily take them apart and move them around as they needed." Mary gives tours of the oldest log cabin in the United States, which was constructed by Jedediah Hyde, Jr., in 1783. He and his wife raised their ten children there, and for more than one hundred fifty years the house was occupied by Hyde descendants. The building is typical of the early homes in this area, built of logs ranging from fourteen to eighteen inches in diameter and consisting of a single room with a massive fieldstone fireplace and a sleeping loft above. The Hyde log cabin is furnished with tools, toys, and household goods mostly from the nineteenth century. It has been completely restored since the Vermont Division for Historic Preservation acquired it in 1952.

Farming is the only industry in the town of Grand Isle, and nearly eighty percent of the total land is either cropland or pasture. Many people commute to neighboring Burlington, the largest city in the state, and to Plattsburgh, New York, to work. The spiffy new one-hundred-eighty-foot *Plattsburgh,* operated by Captain David W. Geer, who has been piloting ferryboats for the Lake Champlain Transportation Company since 1951, was specially built with a reinforced hull to allow it to break through the icy waters of Lake Champlain in the winter.

A fun place to visit is the **Hooting Owl Gift Shop** on Ferry Road, which is run by Frank and Lynda Clark. "We carry everything from Russian china to Curious Critters and everything in between," says Lynda. Many of the items they sell are made locally, while others are imported. Lynda refers to all her carefully chosen items by their creators' names — "Nancy's Limited Editions" or "Lucy's pillows."

"Sometimes we get a little crazy around here, especially by Christmas time," she says, "and we offer special discounts to people for hooting like an owl or getting another customer to join them in a round of 'Jingle Bells.' One time we offered a discount to anyone who would do their college cheer, and we had a '73 Princeton grad running up and down the aisles doing an entire Princeton routine!" They gave him a good discount!

"One time we offered a discount to anyone who would do their college cheer, and we had a '73 Princeton grad running up and down the aisles doing an entire Princeton routine!"

Camping is very popular throughout the Vermont islands. There are several excellent campgrounds on South Hero, some privately run but many part of the Vermont State Parks and Forest Recreation Service. **Grand Isle State Park** is one of the largest, with 156 campsites, 31 of which have lean-tos. The grounds are well-kept, and there are hot showers, flush toilets, and public phones. Each campsite has its own picnic table and fireplace, and you can purchase wood at the registration office. The campground is on the lake and offers swimming, fishing, boat ramps and rentals, and a recreation program. The program includes nature, bird, and wildflower walks with a naturalist and special activities for children.

Because of the relatively mild climate of the islands many plants, flowers, and trees that are either rare or nonexistent in other parts of Vermont grow here. The same is true of birds such as the Hungarian partridge, cattle egret, bald eagle, and cerulean warbler. Many of the nature programs concentrate on searching out and identifying these unusual species.

ACCESS

SOUTH HERO. Directions: From I-89 take exit 17 to Route 2, crossing the Sand Bar Bridge to South Hero.

LAKE CHAMPLAIN TRANSPORTATION COMPANY (Ferry to New York). Directions: Follow Route 2 north from South Hero to Grand Isle and Route 314. Turn right onto Route 314 and follow signs to the ferry landing (on left). **Season:** Year-round. **Admission:** Charged. **Telephone:** (802) 372-5550.

ALLENHOLM FARM. Directions: Follow Route 2 to South Street intersection. Go left onto South Street, and the farm is about a mile down the road on your right.

Visitors are welcome only for special events such as the air show. **Admission:** Free.

CONTENTMENT FARM, INC. Directions: Located 1¼ miles off Route 2 (after crossing Sand Bar Bridge). Go left onto South Street and then left onto East Shore Road. The farm is on your left. **Season:** Year-round. **Admission:** Charged for rides and lessons. **Telephone:** (802) 373-4087.

ISLAND COUNTRY QUILTS. Directions: From Route 2 take a left onto South Street. The shop is about a quarter of a mile along on the left. **Telephone:** (802) 372-4568.

APPLE FARM MARKET. Directions: About a mile past the Sand Bar Bridge, on the left side of Route 2. **Season:** Year-round. **Telephone:** (802) 372-6611.

POST AND BEAM. Directions: On Route 2 in South Hero center. **Season:** Year-round. **Telephone:** (802) 372-5749.

GRAND ISLE. Directions: Follow Route 2 north from South Hero.

HYDE LOG CABIN. Directions: Located on Route 2 about 2 miles past the turnoff for Route 314. The cabin is on your right. **Season:** Memorial Day to mid-October. **Admission:** Donation.

HOOTING OWL GIFT SHOP. Directions: Follow Route 2 north to Route 314. Turn left onto Route 314 and follow the signs toward the ferry landing. The shop is on your left. **Season:** Year-round. **Telephone:** (802) 372-5433.

GRAND ISLE STATE PARK. Directions: From Grand Isle center on Route 2 continue north about 3 miles. Entrance sign and road are on your right. **Season:** Memorial Day through Labor Day weekend. **Admission:** Charged. **Telephone:** (802) 372-4300.

LAKE CHAMPLAIN ISLANDS CHAMBER OF COMMERCE. North Hero, VT 05474; (802) 928-8354.

North Hero

If you sample both restaurants, you'll probably be hard pressed to pick a favorite.

The town of North Hero, the Grand Isle county seat, is where most of the tourists to the islands bed down for the night. Numerous campsites, resort motels, and lodges and a few nice old inns are located on this narrow slip of an island, with gorgeous sunrises to the east and breathtaking sunsets to the west. Few of these facilities are visible from Route 2, except for the two that have exceptional restaurants — **Shore Acres** and **North Hero House.** Both of these establishments, popular with local people and boaters who tie up at the docks on the restaurants'

Nowadays the North Hero Firemen's Roast Beef Dinner is such a popular event that it takes "four settin's" to serve everybody.

waterfronts, pride themselves on their garden-fresh vegetables, fish "right out of the lake," and home-baked pastries. If you sample both restaurants, you'll probably be hard pressed to pick a favorite between the cozy maple dining room overlooking the lake at Shore Acres and the cheery flower-filled solarium at North Hero House.

Another popular overnight spot, the **White Gables Inn,** run by Don and Judy Hard, has a thriving colonial herb garden that takes up its entire front yard. Judy learned the art of growing and cooking with herbs from her mother, who is a noted herbalist and lecturer. Along with selling herbs, making potpourri, and teaching and lecturing about herbs, Judy enjoys tracking down Victorian furnishings for the inn. "We have a very special Victorian Christmas here," she says, "complete with decorations, a large tree right in that corner, and a dinner with all the fixings — from turkey to plum pudding." Guests have come from far and wide — "Paris, England, and recently a woman from Holland," Judy says, noting that this widespread clientele comes "just from people recommending the inn to one another." "Guests quite often ask for a certain room," she adds, and you won't find this surprising once you've seen how each room is uniquely decorated with charming antique furniture and draperies. With cross-country skiing and ice fishing right at their front door, the Hards' guests enjoy the winter just as much as the summer.

The population of North Hero is small, fewer

Smugglers would carry their small boats and booty across The Carry in an attempt to outwit the larger vessels full of federal agents who were close at their heels.

than four hundred fifty at the last census, but community enthusiasm runs high. The annual **North Hero Firemen's Roast Beef Dinner** held in mid-August draws not only most of the townspeople but also many folks from the surrounding towns. "The town hall only holds so many, ya know," an older volunteer said, "and the numbers increase every year. We have to have four settin's now."

Driving north through North Hero, you come to a narrow neck of land that almost cuts the island in two. It's called **The Carry** because Indians were known to carry their canoes from one side to the other to save themselves from paddling around the island. As the islands were settled, fishermen used The Carry to get from one good fishing spot to another more quickly. Its fame — or infamy — was heightened by the Embargo Act of 1807, which made trading with Canada illegal. Smugglers would carry their small boats and booty across The Carry in an attempt to outwit the larger vessels full of federal agents who were close on their heels.

A restaurant called **Birdland** is a perfect place to have breakfast or a light meal. A good supply of Vermont maple products are for sale here, along with some interesting shells, which the owners bring back each year from Florida.

Charlie's Northland Lodge is one of the few places on the islands that offers year-round accommodations. Naturally it is popular with those who like winter sports such as ice fishing, hunting, and cross-country skiing. Charlie can supply most of your needs, including a fishing license. There are tennis courts on the premises, which are available free to guests and for an hourly fee to the public.

ACCESS

NORTH HERO. Directions: Follow Route 2 north from Grand Isle.

SHORE ACRES. Directions: Located on Route 2. Follow the signs. **Season:** Mid-May to mid-October. **Telephone:** (802) 372-8722 or (winter) 372-5545.

NORTH HERO HOUSE. Directions: Follow Route 2 to the center of the village, and the inn (main house) is on your left. (There are also 3 large guesthouses.) **Season:** Mid-June through Labor Day. **Telephone:** (802) 372-8237.

WHITE GABLES INN. Directions: From Route 2, after crossing The Carry, take the right fork in the road. This is Lakeview Drive. The inn is a short way down the road on your left. **Season:** Year-round. **Telephone:** (802) 372-8319.

BIRDLAND. Directions: Located on Route 2 at The Carry (right side of the road). **Season:** June through September. **Telephone:** (802) 372-4220.

CHARLIE'S NORTHLAND LODGE. Directions: On Route 2 in the heart of North Hero village. **Season:** Year-round. **Telephone:** (802) 372-8822.

LAKE CHAMPLAIN ISLANDS CHAMBER OF COMMERCE. North Hero, VT 05474; (802) 928-8354.

Isle La Motte

Nestled on the shore of Vermont's westernmost island, Isle La Motte, is the serenely beautiful **St. Anne's Shrine.** Thousands of visitors come to this peaceful spot each year not only to participate in Feast Day celebrations held several times each summer and to attend the daily outdoor Mass, but also to enjoy the recreational facilities the island has to offer.

Isle La Motte's granite statue of Samuel de Champlain honors the renowned French explorer who discovered, in 1609, the lake that is now named for him.

Isle La Motte was the first island Samuel de Champlain spotted as he sailed into the lake that now bears his name, and it eventually became the first white settlement in Vermont. The French built a fort here in 1666, calling it Fort St. Anne, and celebrated the first Catholic Mass in Vermont on the banks of the lake.

The fort itself was short-lived, but the area has continued to hold a special religious significance, not only for Catholics, but for people of all faiths. Today St. Anne's Shrine occupies most of the site of the former fort, sharing the area with a grotto, a recessed structure housing a statue of the Virgin Mother; Way of the Cross, a circular path commemorating the death of Christ; a marble statue of St. Anne; and a large open-air structure where the daily outdoor Mass is celebrated.

Even if you are not of the Catholic faith, you should have no trouble following the informal Sunday morning Mass service. Many Canadians attend Mass here, so the service is bilingual. The hymns are sung in both French and English, and the congregants actively participate in the service.

A large recreation area surrounding the shrine contains a sandy beach, picnic tables, and a large dock for people who come by boat. A cafeteria with a small store and a gift shop is located nearby.

Close to the site where Champlain is said to have landed in 1609 stands an enormous granite

Amid all this beauty and tranquility, the portrayal of this founding father in such colossal dimensions seems only natural.

statue of him, sculptured at Expo '67 in Montreal. Some historians have mocked the size of the statue, noting that Champlain was of slight build. But amid all this beauty and tranquility, the portrayal of this founding father in such colossal dimensions seems only natural.

Isle La Motte also is known for its quarries of fine, jet-black marble, the first quarries to be worked in Vermont. The quarries still operate today (they are not open to visitors), although demand for such decorative marble has diminished. This special marble has added distinction to many prominent buildings, including the Capitol Building in Washington, D.C., and Radio City Music Hall in New York City.

Only about four hundred year-round residents live on the island, and while farming is still important, most people have out-of-town jobs, some commuting as far as fifty miles.

Isle La Motte has a pretty little village area with a general store, fire station, town hall, Methodist church (with a list of activities a mile long), and library. The library is made of blue-gray stone quarried on the island in the nineteenth century, and throughout the islands you will see many other fine old houses and buildings made from this native material.

Ruthcliffe Lodge, which recently added motel units to its facility, is known in the area for its wonderful food, and anyone who enjoys the sport of fishing will certainly be in his or her element here. Off the beaten track and situated right on the lake, the lodge puts boats and motors at your doorstep, and the perch, pike, and bass are just waiting for you to cast the bait.

ACCESS

ISLE LA MOTTE. Directions: Follow Route 2 north from North Hero. At the junction of South Alburg, take a left turn onto Route 129, crossing a small bridge onto Isle La Motte.

ST. ANNE'S SHRINE. Directions: After crossing the bridge to Isle La Motte, continue south on Route 129, following signs to the shrine. **Season:** May 15 to October 15. **Admission:** Free. **Telephone:** (802) 928-3362 or 928-3385.

RUTHCLIFFE LODGE AND MOTEL RESORT. Directions: From the village of Isle La Motte look for the Ruthcliffe sign about 2 miles past the general store. Turn left and stay on the road to the end. **Season:** May 15 to September 15. **Telephone:** (802) 928-3200.

INDEX

About the Author

WESTWOOD STUDIOS

Born in Connecticut, the youngest in a family of seven daughters, Mary Maynard "learned early on that the best way to get someone's attention was to write them a note or letter." A lifelong New Englander and full-time free-lance writer since 1981, she has traveled extensively in the U.S. and abroad, including trips to Germany, Italy, Great Britain, China, the Soviet Union, Israel, the Caribbean, and scores of U.S. islands.

Her articles on a variety of topics have appeared in *Ms., Boston* magazine, *Equal Times, Sojourner,* and many other periodicals. She is also the author, with her daughter, Mary-Lou Dow, of *Hassle-Free Boston,* a critically acclaimed guide to that city for women. She lives with her husband, Jim, in Weston, Massachusetts, and is the mother of three grown daughters.